FALLEN
WOMAN

ALLISON MANN
WITH LINDA MAY SPENCER AND EMILY JEAN

HADLEIGH HOUSE
PUBLISHING

Hadleigh House Publishing
Minneapolis, MN
www.hadleighhouse.com

Cover design by Alisha Perkins

ISBN-978-1-7357738-3-4
ISBN-978-1-7357738-4-1 (ebook)
LCCN: 2021906297

To anyone who's ever fallen…

There is nothing left for me here.

Three slices.

One, two, three.

One on top of the other, starting at my wrist.

No one wants me.

My family is gone.

I'm completely alone.

This will be better for everyone. Maybe I'll see Mom.

If she went there. If I go, there.

There are broken pieces everywhere. Mementos, symbols.

Of what?

They mean more smashed and broken … like my life.

Like me.

I'm getting tired now. I've always been tired.

Tired of living, tired of needing, craving, fighting, fleeing.

If I fall now, I won't get up. If I fall now, I won't wake.

I'll be gone.

Gone from all of this.

Is this what I want?

Blood is dripping from my arm … running down, staining the floor.

Blood stains are how my life began.

Will they be how I end?

If I fall asleep, I will not return. But if I don't? If I fight to stay, if I change my mind …

Can anybody catch me?

Will I ever be more, more than broken?

More than fallen?

INTRODUCTION

LINDA IS NOTHING LIKE I expected, and yet exactly what I imagined. She walked into the coffee shop for our first meeting dressed in blue jeans and a bomber jacket. At first blush I thought, *Nope, not her.* Then I noticed the beautiful, young woman next to her, the one who had first reached out to me—her daughter, Emily.

When you get that kind of email, you do your research. "My mother owned and operated two saunas/brothels in Saint Paul, Minnesota, from 1976 until a very controversial and publicized court case in 1997, when she had to eventually close her doors," Emily's email had begun.

I vividly remember reading that message and immediately opening Google. "Linda May Spencer, MN," I typed. The search didn't return much. A 1993 Minnesota Court of Appeals case, *City of Saint Paul v. Spencer*, was all I could find. As a long-time paralegal in the Twin Cities, I recognized more than one of the names listed in the case, both lawyers and judges. The case was about a public nuisance dispute in the city of Saint Paul. I saw the facts of the case mentioned prostitution and misdemeanor convictions, and my interest was piqued.

Not seeing much more in my Google search, I moved on. Social media being the next logical place to find out more about the woman who had emailed me, and her potentially felonious mother, I jumped on Facebook. Once again, there wasn't much to find, but what I could see was a profile picture of a woman named Emily Jean.

So, there I sat, an email message, a court case, and a photo. This information conjured images and scenarios in my mind, as it would anyone's: Heidi Fleiss, *Moulin Rouge!*, fur coats, diamonds, and of course my personal favorite, *Pretty Woman*.

It was important that I'd been able to confirm a few things: Emily existed, a woman named Linda May Spencer had owned and operated saunas in Saint Paul, and there had indeed been a court case. It wouldn't hurt to meet them and find out more.

Sitting in the coffee shop waiting for Linda and her

daughter was surreal. I looked up every time the door opened. I'm certain I appeared as if I were waiting for a blind date to arrive. I was nervous, excited, and just a little bit scared. Who was I about to meet?

I felt my excitement rising as the woman in the bomber jacket and her daughter walked toward the table. This lady may not have been famous, but there was certainly potential that she was infamous. I couldn't wait to learn more.

From the moment she sat down and started talking, it was clear that Linda May Spencer had lived life. Her voice was hoarse and gravelly, her eyes dark with experience. What she lacked in glitz and glamor, she made up for in grit and wisdom. If I had been unsure of the legitimacy of the story I read in that first email from Emily, all unease fell away in the first ten minutes of meeting Linda.

Emily sat next to her mother quietly at first. She listened as we talked and prompted her mother from time to time on details she'd left out. I didn't hear the whole story that night—time wouldn't allow—but Linda painted a picture in broad strokes. She had been a wife, a mother, and a businesswoman, not unlike me, but just below the surface was a long, dark tale that would take twists and turns almost impossible to believe.

I wanted to learn more about Linda May Spencer. I wanted to know her daughter and hear what it was like to grow up with a mother who owned brothels. I wanted to use my knowledge of the law and the courts, my skills in investigation and interviewing, but most importantly, I wanted to tell this story. I wanted to open the long-shelved files in the courthouses and city halls, the police files and memories of the people who lived through this, and piece it all together.

I wanted to tell the story of Linda May Spencer, a woman who had fallen, a fallen woman who, remarkably, sat across the table from me in a coffee shop that night and began telling me how she got up.

For the next year, I spent hours with Linda. I learned about her story, her business and her family. But, I did more than just listen, I researched. I searched databases, libraries, courthouses and police files. I read transcripts, court documents and reports unlike anything I had seen before. From her narrative and those of others who documented the events in real time, I've been able to weave together this remarkable portrait of a woman and a time rarely talked about today.

Many of the events in this book may be difficult to read. The impact of the struggles, the crimes and the trauma cannot be fully conveyed without honoring the truth and the darkness within them. In many cases, names have been changed, as indicated by an asterisk, to protect the privacy of those involved. Often times, women involved in sex-for-money transactions used an alias they had chosen as a "work name." These names have not been changed.

Reports from the Saint Paul Police Department contained detailed and often graphic documentation of the events which occurred. Much of the dialogue in this book is taken directly from reports as written. In a few instances, dialogue was derived from narrative presented in the reports.

■ ■ ■

DOWNTOWN SAINT PAUL IS quiet. It has an old, slow feeling about it. As you walk the streets of the city, you can look around and see history. Cornerstones mark dates of construction back to the 1800s, while brick buildings with tall, still-intact archways lead to libraries, museums, and theaters. Saint Paul thrives with Midwestern culture and boasts a rich history.

The capitol city of the State of Hockey has many claims to fame, including F. Scott Fitzgerald, Charles Schulz, and perhaps most important, Saint Paul, Minnesota, is the birthplace of Scotch tape. And while you can tour Saint Paul, greeting Lucy, Linus, and good ole Charlie Brown, what you don't see on the corners, in the buildings, or in any storefronts is a history far different than cartoons and Post-it Notes.

While Herb Brooks coached his hockey team, while the Minnesota Twins won two World Series, and while the famous Mall of America was being built just a few miles down the road, a dark, secret industry was thriving in the city of Saint Paul, and officials were desperately trying to shut it down.

Throughout history, many monikers have been given to buildings where one could go and pay money to have sex. In today's world, we are familiar with terms like "bunny ranch" and "whorehouse," but dating back to the early history of the United States, and specifically Saint Paul, these buildings were called "houses of ill repute," "bordellos," "brothels," and "massage parlors." But as society and laws evolved, so did locations formally tucked away in red-light districts and hidden alleyways.

In the early 1960s in Saint Paul through the end of the 1990s, a person wanting to purchase sex need only look for a "sauna" or "health club" to satisfy his desire. Storefront saunas were located all around the city, and inside them an illegal business thrived.

PART 1

CHAPTER 1

WALTER SPENCER RACED UP the Santa Monica Freeway. He had to strike the perfect balance between speed and stability. The blood bank gave him just enough to transfuse his newborn daughter, Linda May, but he needed to get the pouches there fast. The baby had been born hours earlier, and the doctors said she needed a full blood replacement. Because Linda and her mother had incompatible blood types, her mother's blood had transferred antibodies through the placenta that were now attacking the baby's red blood cells. Linda was being poisoned by her mother's blood. He had to get there in time, or the baby wouldn't make it.

Arriving back at the hospital, Walter ran to his trunk to get the pouches of blood to bring to the doctors. He had made it in record time. He knew as he opened the trunk that he would always be credited for saving his daughter's life. He liked that.

Now, there were blood stains in the fabric of Walter's trunk. Tiny little spots of dark red soaked into the carpeted space. If someone didn't know to look, they would never even notice the spots, but Walter would. He would always know when he looked at those spots that it was Linda who ruined his car.

Walter Spencer stands next to his station wagon. Courtesy of Linda May Spencer.

■ ■ ■

TALL, DARK, AND HANDSOME, Walter Spencer was thirty years older than his wife, Margaret. She had easily fallen for his piercing green eyes and British accent when she and her girlfriends arrived in Los Angeles from Saint Paul a few years prior.

Margaret had been in search of sun, sand, and Hollywood; she found all of that and more in Walter. He was a bit-part actor and loved to talk about himself. Walter had spent his life using his looks and personality to win people over. He may have been a conman, lying about being everything from a chiropractor to a professional boxer, but Margaret didn't see it. She fell in love, and they were married not long after they met·

Margaret Spencer with five of her children. Courtesy of Linda May Spencer.

Linda was the third child born to Walter and Margaret Spencer, but she was not the last. In total, the couple had six children together prior to Walter's death in 1956.

■ ■ ■

AFTER HER ENTRANCE INTO the world, Linda Spencer continued to have a rough life. Her birth had been traumatic, causing both a lack of oxygen to her infant brain and the need for a total blood transfusion. Because of this, Linda suffered a number of neurological problems. Not only did she have difficulty in school due to learning disabilities, she also suffered physical setbacks. Nerve damage caused Linda to have an uncontrollable jerk in her arm. Without warning, her arm would flail into the air, oftentimes causing a disruption around her. Kids at school teased her constantly, and she was, without intent, a distraction in her classrooms.

While Linda's mother did seek help for her daughter by way of special schools and medical treatment, she never explained to young Linda what it was that made her different. Margaret would take Linda to doctor's offices for treatments, leaving her there alone with the doctors and nurses. She did not stay to comfort her young child or explain what it was that would be happening to her; she simply left her frightened child with the doctor. Linda never understood why her body moved in the ways that it did, different from the other kids, or why she sometimes had trouble understanding things in school. Where a mother could have educated her child to help comprehend and accept her differences, Margaret left Linda to wonder.

Margaret was cold. She never offered comfort or love to her children. While she provided for them in the form of food and shelter, she did not wipe their tears or care for them when they were ill. She did not share things with her children or talk with them. Margaret was a secret keeper, always hiding her own feelings and never asking others to share theirs.

CHAPTER 2

NESTLED IN THE HILLS of Malibu, California, was the home where Linda Spencer began her life. The house was no bigger than a shed with a decent-sized yard. It was a tiny space that housed all eight members of the Spencer family. While basic life necessities were provided for the Spencer children, they did not have the things other children their age did. While their friends had toys to play with, Linda and her siblings were given parts of turkey carcasses to keep them entertained. Their father slaughtered turkeys and gave his children the claws with tendons still attached. When Linda pulled on the tendon, the claw would open and close.

While other kids went to school in freshly pressed clothes, Linda recalls many days where she didn't wear underwear under her dress because she didn't have any clean to put on.

Linda May Spencer with her older sister in Malibu, CA. Courtesy of Linda May Spencer.

For his part as a father, Walter Spencer did not pay much mind to his children. Linda's memories of her father are limited, recalling him drunk more often than sober and heavy-handed with her mother. She remembers a particularly scary experience when her father lit her mother's bathrobe on fire after tying her to a chair. Linda and her siblings watched in panic as their father laughed at their screaming mother. When he left the room, Linda's older brother put out the fire and untied their mom. No one ever spoke of it again. Linda grew up fearing her father rather than respecting him.

Walter's main goal in life was to become a Hollywood actor and, in the absence of that, he used alcohol to fill his emptiness. From time to time, Linda can remember her father getting bit parts on television, once acting as a judge in a courtroom scene. She remembers Walter making all of his children sit to watch as his big moment flashed on the television. He was so proud of himself and demanded the same pride from his children, although Linda in particular was hard-pressed to give it to him.

Walter did many frightening things in the eyes of his children. Linda remembers his violent treatment of animals that would come into their yard in California. If Walter was outside when a cat made its way onto their property, he would lure the cat in. After calling to his children to come see the cat, Walter would hold it underwater in the small kiddie pool that sat under the tree in the backyard. Once the cat stopped breathing, Walter would hang it from the clothesline for the family to see.

Contrary to how her father wished it to be, there was no fame or fortune in the Spencer family's Malibu life. Eventually, Walter's drinking caught up to him, and in 1956, when Linda was five years old, he died. There was no fanfare when she lost her father. Margaret had taken all of the children to the hospital one evening. Linda remembers seeing her father in the bed—he was completely yellow. Her mother told her and her siblings to say goodbye, and so they did. Linda did not understand that this was the kind of goodbye that would last forever; she didn't know her father would never come home. She said goodbye as if it were goodnight and never saw her father again.

■ ■ ■

ALTHOUGH THERE WAS NO more abuse, no more yelling, and no more drinking in the house, things did not improve. Suddenly finding herself the single mother of six children was difficult for Margaret. She needed to find work to support herself and her children. Eventually she found her way to the police academy in Los Angeles and began taking classes.

Once she graduated from the academy, Margaret began looking for work. Being a rookie and a woman led her to the only job she could find, a nightshift as a guard at the LA county jail. The work was tough, not only the hours but the physical demands. Margaret was injured many times, once leading to dental surgery and the extraction of nearly all of her teeth.

It was during this time that Margaret herself turned to drinking. Instead of being mean and angry like their father, Margaret would become quiet and sad when she drank. Linda hated seeing her mother with a bottle because she knew that meant her mom was going to disappear into her bedroom for hours and hours.

Margaret Spencer at work at the LA County Jail. Courtesy of Linda May Spencer.

Because of their mother's job, the Spencer children grew up largely unsupervised. Margaret slept during the day, leaving her young children to fend for themselves in the dangerous world of the Hollywood hills. On summer days, they would find their way to the lagoons on the oceanfront or up into the mountains above. Spending days running free was not exciting for Linda. She felt scared and exposed during these times. Linda lived with the constant sense that danger was lurking around every corner.

Linda recalls more than one occasion when she was escorted home as a child by police officers. Busted for running through stores without shoes or playing with matches in the dry underbrush of the forest, Linda and her siblings often found themselves in trouble. The police scolded her mother for allowing her children to run around the way they did, but there wasn't much she could do. She explained to them that she had to work nights to keep food on her table and, because she worked all night, she needed to rest during the day. She knew this wasn't ideal, but it was the only way she could support her children.

Police officers were quick to advise Margaret that leaving her children unsupervised at night and allowing them to run like they did during the day could lead to the county taking them away from her. So, Margaret was forced to find a babysitter who would take the youngest five children at night, where they would be safe while she worked. This would alleviate at least part of the risk she was taking while trying to provide for her family.

Every night on her way to work, Margaret would drop her five youngest children at the home of a woman she barely knew. Before the days of licensing or background checks, Margaret had no choice but to trust the woman to keep her children safe. The babysitter had a live-in boyfriend who would also be there when Linda and her siblings arrived at night. This man was big with blond hair, and he smelled terrible. While the babysitter herself spoke mostly Spanish with the occasional broken English, her boyfriend was easy to understand.

Seven-year-old Linda understood every word he muttered as he lay on top of her, night after night. She knew exactly what he said as he whispered in her ear, "I will kill you," while he forced his body inside of hers. She knew what he did was wrong, she knew that no one would come to help her, but she also knew that if she told, life would just get harder for everyone else.

⊞ ⊞ ⊞

THERE WAS NO SENSE of security in Linda's life. She never felt safe or loved during her time in California. Life was chaotic and scary all of the time. But there was one person in her life she could count on, one source of ease among the tension. This was her oldest brother, Walter Spencer, Jr., nicknamed "Abby" by his family. Perhaps it was the years between them or his calm demeanor that made Linda feel so safe, but she always knew when Abby was around, things would be okay. She loved being close to him whenever she could, watching him play baseball games or hanging around him at home.

By the time Linda was eight years old, Abby was suddenly scarce. Weeks would go by without Abby coming home, and when he was home, he was in his room alone. She constantly asked her mom where her brother was, and he was always somewhere else, at a friend's house, at baseball, on a trip for school. Linda hated when he was gone. Abby was the only male in Linda's life whom she truly trusted. He had become a security blanket for her, and without him, she felt helpless.

Linda was about nine years old when her mother told her and her siblings they would be moving to Saint Paul to live with their grandmother. Linda was relieved. Even at such a young age, she understood that moving away meant stopping the abuse she was suffering at the hands of the babysitter's boyfriend, and she looked forward to being cared for by her grandmother. For Linda, this was a great hope for her life to start getting better. Maybe Abby wouldn't play baseball when they moved. Maybe he wouldn't be with his friends so much because all of his friends would still be living in California.

But when Margaret Spencer and her six children got on the plane headed east, she kept one life-changing secret from them. Although Linda and four of her siblings traveled together on the plane, their oldest brother was noticeably absent.

"Where is Abby?" Linda asked her mother on the plane.

"Don't worry about it," her mother told her.

It would be months before Linda heard about her brother Abby. Linda and her siblings were taking classes at the Catholic church to receive their first communion. Their grandmother had required this as a condition of Margaret bringing her children to Saint Paul to live with her. During a class, Linda spoke to a nun about her family and talked about her favorite person in the whole world, her big brother, Abby. One day, Sister Mary Delores sat the Spencer children down under a tree outside of the church in Saint Paul and told Linda and her siblings that their brother had died. He had been diagnosed with a brain tumor while they were still living in California.

Linda didn't understand then, but all of those times when Abby was gone, he was in the hospital getting treatment. Her mother had hidden the entire illness from her children. And, as it turned out, Abby *was* on the plane with them that day. He was in a coffin in the cargo hold, in transport to his final resting place in Saint Paul. Linda knows now, as a mother herself, that it was probably the unimaginable grief of losing her son that led Margaret back to Minnesota, back to her own mother, to a place where she wouldn't feel so alone.

The Saint Paul home where Margeret Spencer and her children lived with her mother. Courtesy of Linda May Spencer.

CHAPTER 3

DESPITE HER GREAT HOPES, life was not better for young Linda in Minnesota. Her mother continued to work as a police officer, and she was forced to live with her mean and nasty grandmother until they were able to get a house on their own. Where she had previously been left to roam free, now Linda was under the forceful hand of a grandmother who was strict and oftentimes physical with Linda and her siblings.

Linda and her brother and sisters attended Garlough Elementary School in Saint Paul. This was a big change from the special school that Linda went to in California.

Now she was with the "regular" kids, and she was expected to learn and act like they did. Linda struggled, but no one seemed to notice. She muddled her way through classwork, getting average grades without specific help for her learning disabilities or physical differences.

There was never anyone in the Spencer home checking in on the children. Linda didn't come home from school to a mom asking if she had any homework. She rarely even brought home a book. No one encouraged her to try hard or do her schoolwork; she just did what the teachers told her to do. No one ever asked Linda what she wanted to be when she grew up or gave her any direction in looking toward the future. Linda skated through school largely unnoticed.

At Henry Sibley High School in Saint Paul, Linda Spencer found friends. She'd been somewhat of a loner in elementary school, sticking to her siblings and rarely interacting with the other children. In high school, this changed. While she didn't fit in with the preppy or smart kids, Linda found a home with the troublemakers, the kids who skipped class and smoked marijuana under the bleachers at the football games.

By this time, Margaret had moved her children into a home not too far from their grandmother, but the teenagers were free to come and go as they pleased. Margaret rarely paid much attention to their whereabouts. To her, it was only important that they went to school every day and, once they were old enough, got a job. For the most part, Linda was once again free to roam.

It was during her high school years that Linda met Beth*, who was a kindred spirit. Beth lived in a similar situation with little supervision or direction in her life. Together, Linda and Beth started finding trouble when they were just fourteen years old.

Because neither of them had someone at home paying attention to what they were doing, Linda and Beth could easily sneak out at night. Beth introduced Linda to a way that they could easily earn spending money. She had also introduced Linda to cocaine, so it was soon a necessity that they have money to spend. Late at night, the two girls would sneak out their bedroom windows and meet up halfway between their houses. They would make their way to a bar on West Seventh Street in Saint Paul that featured go-go dancers in cages late into the night. No one ever asked; Linda and Beth would just jump in and start dancing. At the end of the night, they would collect all of the money that had been thrown in the cages and head home. For the young high school women, this was a lucrative venture. No one ever seemed to care that they snuck out of their houses or into the bar; no one ever asked their age. They just did what they did and went home.

It was also with Beth that Linda found herself attending dances at the Prom Ballroom. The massive event center was a place like none other in Saint Paul during its time. With a lounge and bandstand, it was *the* place to go. Acts like Glenn Miller, Frank Sinatra, and the Everly Brothers all made appearances at the Prom Ballroom.

Linda and Beth spent a lot of time at the Ballroom, sneaking drinks from older friends, doing drugs in the parking lot, and dancing the night away to whatever band happened to be playing. Sixteen-year-old Linda fell head over heels for a singing guitar player who graced the stage one particular evening. She found him after his set and learned that he was twenty years old and a teacher at a school across the river in Wisconsin. Despite their age difference, Linda and the guitar player struck up a romance. He would come to Saint Paul on the weekends and take Linda on dates. Together, they had big dreams of a big future.

Linda was only sixteen years old when she found out the singing guitar player had gotten her pregnant. It was devastating news. She knew without a doubt that if she told her mother, she would be kicked out of the house. Linda was terrified.

With no place to turn, she looked to friends for advice. One such friend, who had also found herself pregnant, was headed to New York to have an abortion. It was their high school social studies teacher who had made all of her arrangements, and Linda asked for assistance, as well. The two young women flew together to New York City, where they both had abortions.

When she returned from her trip, Linda became extremely ill. Her mother barged into her bedroom one morning when Linda did not get up for school. She was in too much pain and was too weak to get out of bed.

She knew something had gone wrong with the abortion, but she was terrified to tell her mother. As her mother whipped her with a police belt for not going to school, Linda wept. She couldn't possibly tell her mother why she was so ill, but she couldn't manage to pull herself from her bed, either. Finally, her mother realized that Linda was quite sick and took her to the doctor. Once in the safety of the doctor's office, Linda was able to get help. She received a procedure to remove the infected remnants of her pregnancy, and her mother was never informed about what had happened.

Linda eventually graduated from Saint Paul's Henry Sibley High School. She wasn't the first in her class, but she also wasn't the last. After all of her struggles, it had been a remarkable accomplishment for Linda to receive her diploma. After graduation, she tried taking the path of others her age and signed up for classes at a small technical college in the southern suburbs of the Twin Cities. She was adept at acting and speaking, excelling in her debate and public speaking classes. But while she didn't hate her classes, Linda realized quickly there was no path to making big money in a career she would find from staying in school. Linda wanted to make big money.

■ ■ ■

DURING HER HIGH SCHOOL years, Linda learned a lot about life from her friend Beth. With thoughts of college in her rearview, Linda looked to Beth for guidance on how to make a living. By this time, Beth was living in New York City, working in a criminal ring operating a con game. She was earning fast cash doing a pigeon drop con, and as it turned out, Beth was looking for a partner. With the promise of money on the horizon, Linda jumped on a plane to New York to meet up with Beth and learn how to work a con.

When she arrived, Linda met up with Beth, and they began working their scam. The game was complicated, but the payout was worth the labor. The women would walk through the upscale department stores of New York City, looking for a mark. Rich, elderly women were the ideal target for a pigeon drop.

Once a mark was identified, Beth would approach her and begin striking up a conversation. At this point, Linda would be standing close by, waiting to pounce. If it appeared that the elderly woman was a good target, Linda would begin her approach. Walking up to the two women now chatting, Linda would hold out a purse.

"Excuse me, I don't mean to interrupt, but did one of you drop this?" she would say.

"No, did you?" Beth would reply, turning to the mark.

The mark would invariably say no, she had not dropped the purse either, at which time Beth would suggest opening the purse to find identification. Upon opening the purse, it would be revealed that there were thousands of dollars of cash inside, but nothing else. Now, Linda would get upset.

"Oh no. What have I done?" she would cry.

Beth would interject, "I work for a lawyer. Why don't I call him and ask what we should do?"

"Okay," Linda would say. The mark, now completely mesmerized by this situation, would continue talking with the women. Beth would walk away as if to find a phone while Linda stayed with the mark, giving her a sob story of how she was a young single mother living in the city, just trying to make ends meet.

Beth would return and tell Linda that her boss said that when someone finds lost money with no means of identification that they can keep the money if they deposit it into a safety deposit box for a set time, along with an amount of collateral or good faith money. Linda would cry, insisting that she couldn't possibly come up with the collateral but needed the money, and what a blessing it would be for her and her child. The mark, who was now deeply entrenched in the situation, would offer to lend Linda the money for the collateral, as long as she paid her back the original amount after she got the money from the purse. Linda would reluctantly accept.

The three women would walk to a bank, where Beth claimed to have access to a safety deposit box via her boss. The mark would give Linda cash to take into the bank for deposit along with the purse, and the three women would exchange information for the return of the money. Oftentimes, Linda and Beth would disappear into the bank never to be seen again. Other times, they would return the woman an envelope that had been filled with paper heavy enough to feel like cash.

The two women got away with this con many times before the inevitable happened. Linda was riding an escalator inside a department store in New York, when suddenly a woman started shouting, "That's her! She stole my money!" After running all the way back to the apartment where she was staying with Beth, Linda decided her time in the pigeon drop was over. She'd paid too much of her earnings to ring bosses, and she was tired. So, at twenty years old, with no job and no prospects, Linda packed her bags and moved back home to Saint Paul.

CHAPTER 4

BACK HOME, LIVING WITH her mother and looking for work, Linda found herself in need of cocaine. After reaching out to some friends, it was suggested to Linda that she head to the Highland Park area of Saint Paul and find a guy named Kenneth Cline, a well-known drug dealer in the area. He would be at the bar wearing corduroy pants and a blue jean jacket. True to legend, when Linda walked in, there was Kenny, tall and handsome with a Fu Manchu and bell-bottoms, sitting at the bar. It wasn't hard for the young, slender, blond-haired Linda Spencer to get drugs from Mr. Cline. He took a liking to her immediately.

It wasn't long after meeting that Linda and Kenny started dating. Linda's interest in Kenny was singular. It wasn't his good looks or success that drew Linda in; it was that he supplied her with endless access to cocaine: she was addicted to him. Linda could get high whenever she wanted with Kenny around and, at that time in her life, this was her main interest.

What Linda didn't immediately know was that Kenny was more than just a drug dealer. He was a drug runner involved in one of the largest cocaine rings in the country. When she moved in with him, Linda realized that his home was literally full of cocaine. There was coke in the kitchen cabinets where plates, cups, and bowls would be stored. Under the sink in the bathroom, where she would expect to find extra rolls of toilet paper, was more coke. This didn't faze Linda. She was happy to live in a home where she had all the drugs she needed. In fact, Linda took on the job of keeping track of and organizing all of the cocaine that came into the house.

Living and partying with Kenny was good, but Linda wanted more in her life. After a while, she decided she would start looking for work of her own. She needed to find some financial independence from Kenny.

When she started looking for work, Linda knew she didn't want a nine-to-five office job. That would bore her. She also knew she couldn't work as a waitress or bartender because even though the jerk in her arm had stopped when she was young, she always worried it would come back.

Linda turned instead to friends she had met while partying with Kenny. These women, who were similarly situated to her, seemed to always have money and were almost always free to party when asked. What she learned was that many of them were working in massage parlors in Saint Paul.

How hard could it be to give a backrub? Linda thought to herself. And so, in the early 1970s, Linda made her way to Saint Paul in search of a job in a massage parlor.

PART 2

CHAPTER 5

It was the 1960s when a new series of businesses began to crop up in the Twin Cities. Storefront saunas quickly became a growing trend. Inside these businesses, a person could find a steam, get a massage, or even take a bath followed by an application of talcum powder to soften the skin. Women were flocking to these businesses for work, and men soon became frequent customers.

At their inception, these businesses were not regulated by any state or local government. The newness of store-front saunas left officials scratching their heads for ways to monitor the trade. Without oversight, the employees and clientele of the saunas and massage parlors were able to take advantage of closed doors and dark rooms to make deals for services not even the owners recognized were being provided.

When it came to light that men were paying for sex inside the rooms of their businesses, owners found ways to capitalize on the sales. Soon, storefront saunas were well known as places to go for not only relaxation but sexual satisfaction. The businesses quickly grew from small-revenue-generating ventures into a million-dollar industry.

The fast rise in popularity drew attention from government officials, and soon lawmakers were looking for opportunities to regulate the industry. The City of Saint Paul took matters into its own hands when the state failed to pass legislation to govern the saunas and massage parlors. By the early 1970s, women working inside these businesses were required to obtain licensure to provide massage services. A license requirement gave the City power to regulate the provision of services, as well as the capacity to prosecute those found to be providing such services without the required license.

Many of the Saint Paul storefront saunas and massage parlors were already operating lucrative businesses when the license requirement was passed. In order to stay open, the owners found themselves scrambling to license their employees as quickly as possible. Joining together, the business owners came up with a class that would allow its students to apply for licensure upon completion and began running their employees through the classes at warp speed. They'd managed to build a class that fit the mandates established by the city, and so women who completed the course were licensed without issue.

■ ■ ■

IN THE EARLY 1970S when Linda was looking for work, she heard through friends that getting a massage license in Saint Paul would be easy, and once she had one, she could work in pretty much any massage parlor or sauna she wanted. Her friends also told her that these jobs paid cash. This was exactly what Linda had been looking for: easy work that paid cash. So, at the end of 1973, she took the short required class and applied for a masseur's license.

Once her license was granted, Linda began filling out applications at various locations around the city. She knew from friends which locations paid the best and which to stay away from, but what she didn't know was that once she was hired, she would be expected to do things that had not been covered in the license class or on the job applications.

Linda was thrilled when she got a call for an interview from Lee Lenore's Sauna on Snelling Avenue in Saint Paul. She heard good things about the owner and was looking forward to making some money of her own. On the day of her interview, Linda sat in a back room of the building across a table from Lenore.

"If he wants a blow job, you can do that. Just tell him he has to pay more," Lenore said.

Linda sat staring, mouth agape. "What?" she asked, barely able to get sound to come from her mouth.

"It's okay. You just charge him more and give him what he wants. Soon, honey, the johns will be lining up asking for you. Just look at ya." Lenore waved theatrically.

Linda looked down at herself. She was wearing white go-go boots and a skirt so short it barely covered her rear end.

"So, here's what you do," Lenore said as she held a pink slip of paper in her hand. "A john comes in, and he tells whoever is workin' up front what he wants. Whoever is on and not busy comes to the front and walks by that window up there. If he likes you—you get the trick."

"Trick?" Linda asked quietly.

"Yeah, honey, you get the trick! He pays for a number one; that means you are gonna give him a hand job. It goes from there, ya know? So, you pay me fifteen bucks for every trick, and you get to keep the rest. Now, I know how long these things take, so don't you go giving out a lay when you only wrote down a blow job—that shit doesn't fly with me. You in there for an hour, and I see a number one on your slip—I'm coming through that door. Got it?" Lenore's tone was serious and stern. Linda was nervous.

"Oh, okay. Yes, got it," she replied.

■ ■ ■

Reluctantly, Linda took the job at Lee Lenore's, but it didn't take long for her to learn that she did not like turning tricks. She didn't know why exactly, but men made her uncomfortable. She didn't like touching them, but, more than that, she didn't like them touching her.

Linda worked on and off at Lee Lenore's for about two years, although it wasn't something she enjoyed doing. Working for cash gave her some freedom from Kenny, but she was still living with him, so she didn't need much to get by. She would work when she felt like earning some money and disappear for a while until she ran out. There were so many women working at Lee Lenore's that it was easy for Linda to just pop in and out whenever she felt like she needed money. She had regulars who would call for her, and when they did, someone would let her know so she could go to the sauna and meet them.

Linda continued working on and off and living with Kenny until December 9, 1975, when he was arrested for his involvement in a "large-scale cocaine smuggling ring."[1] Linda and Kenny were in bed sleeping when she was startled awake by voices yelling to "Get up," and "Put your hands in the air!" Opening her eyes to the dark metal of guns held by multiple police officers, Linda was terrified. She had no idea what was happening or how the police had gotten into her bedroom but soon she was being told to get dressed and led to the living room where she would sit on the couch

1 Doug Stone, "Drug Agents Bust Big Cocaine Ring, *Star Tribune,* December 10, 1975.

while the officers questioned Kenny in the bedroom. As she sat quietly, guarded by an officer, Linda wondered how the police had gotten past the couple's three large and loud dogs.

The officers took Kenny and Linda into custody that night. Although she was not directly involved with the cocaine ring, Linda had unknowingly spoken to undercover agents about the drug activity just a few days earlier at a party. Linda was charged with possession of amphetamines but never indicted on cocaine charges.

With Kenny in jail, Linda quickly realized she had nothing. Her life had become isolated with Kenny. She hadn't needed friends outside of his. She didn't need her own car or a place to live because Kenny gave her all of that. She was high all of the time and just went along with whatever he had told her to do. It wasn't a glamorous life, but she had what she needed. Now, she had nothing without him. Thankfully, she had taken the job at Lee Lenore's, so she had some work experience, if nothing else.

Linda needed to start making more money and working more shifts than she was getting at Lenore's, so she started to look for other places to work. This was when Linda found the Civic Center Sauna closer to downtown Saint Paul. She first started by picking up shifts at Civic Center, but after a while, she was working there full time.

Linda got to know the owners and managers at the Civic Center well, and after working there for about a year, she started taking on management duties. Soon, Linda was enjoying working as a sauna manager much more than she enjoyed turning tricks. She was learning the inner workings of the business and getting to know some of the owners and operators of other local saunas through a group of owners that had begun working together in a fight against the City of Saint Paul.

■ ■ ■

STOREFRONT SAUNAS WERE QUICKLY growing in popularity not just in Minnesota, but all over the country, as property and business owners learned ways around laws and regulations that increased their bottom line. When the owner of the Civic Center Sauna found himself jilted by his longtime love, he decided he wanted to make a move. As a pilot, he felt that he had an ideal opportunity to expand his business westward, and he asked Linda to manage a new sauna for him.

Linda accompanied the owner to Seattle on a trip to scout locations. While she was there, it became apparent that the man was not only looking for a manager; he was also looking for a girlfriend, and she was not interested. When she returned home, Linda went back to turning tricks and managing the Civic Center Sauna.

But Linda had gotten a taste of what it would be like to own and operate a business rather than to work for one. She liked it. She saw the freedom the owners had to do as they pleased and the fast money they earned.

While she continued working at the sauna, Linda started thinking about what she could do to build her own business. She even went so far as to start creating a fashion show business, but the fruits of her labor never paid off.

CHAPTER 6

YEARS EARLIER, WHILE SHE was working at Lee Lenore's, Linda had met a man who had wanted to take care of her. Clarence was a regular john who had grown to adore Linda. He was thirty-two years older than her, a successful sod farmer from the northern suburb of White Bear Lake. Clarence had followed Linda when she moved to the Civic Center Sauna and continued to come in and see her quite often.

Back when she first met Clarence, Linda hadn't been in need of a sugar daddy. She knew from other women working in saunas that having a rich man to take care of you meant freedom from a lot of worry, but Linda was with Kenny. She didn't need Clarence's money; she had Kenny taking care of everything she needed. But now, seeing Clarence reminded Linda there was another way to be taken care of, and soon, she found herself reconsidering the offer from years ago.

Clarence was still rich and single. When Linda told him about what happened with Kenny, he was happy to offer her a place to live on his farm. She was hesitant, at first, to accept his offer. She wasn't certain she wanted to live with a man again. Linda wanted Clarence's money, not to have a romantic or domestic relationship with him. But when she found out Clarence intended for her to move into an empty home on his farmland, she was thrilled at the idea.

Linda and Clarence never had a romantic relationship. They were an odd couple not only in their age difference but in their stature as well. Linda was small, petite by any measure, and beautiful while Clarence was tall and broad, a farmer through and through, with a plain face and rough hands. He came from hard work and a country upbringing and she was a city girl, rough around the edges and street-wise from experience.

Clarence's farm wasn't close to the city, but he bought Linda a car so she could continue to work at the sauna and visit her family in Saint Paul. Clarence bought Linda many lavish things, from a horse to ride at the farm to jewelry and fancy handbags. She truly had everything she needed and more while she was with Clarence·

There was one thing, though, that Linda kept secret from Clarence: her cocaine use. She felt that if Clarence knew she used drugs, he would be disappointed in her. She worried he might not take care of her if he knew what she spent her money on. While he gave her food, shelter, and many comforts, Linda still needed to make money to support her drug use, so she continued working at the sauna.

Linda was living a relatively easy life financially, but there was something deep down that plagued her. She still hated turning tricks. For some of the women it was easy; they enjoyed the sex, they got so high they didn't notice, or they had some ability to turn themselves off while they worked, but for Linda, it wasn't so easy. Even high on cocaine, Linda could not block out the sense of terror she felt when she was with a john. So, she became adept at making a man believe she was sexually satisfying him without allowing him to touch her. She convinced johns that looking at her was sexually arousing and found ways to keep them coming back for more without allowing herself to feel the pain of her past. And while she didn't particularly care for the work she was doing, Linda was making fast money, and that was what she needed to support her drug use.

By September of 1976, with a boyfriend in jail and a sugar daddy who knew nothing about her drug use, Linda decided to stay in the business and renew her massage license. Clarence had mentioned a number of times that he had considered investing in a sauna location. As a customer, he knew the draw, and as a businessman, he saw the value. Linda began talking with him about the things she had learned from working at Lee Lenore's and managing at the Civic Center Sauna. She told Clarence that if he made the decision to buy a sauna, she would be the perfect person to run it.

CHAPTER 7

LEE LENORE'S WAS NOT the first or the only massage parlor in Saint Paul in the 1970s. By the middle of the twentieth century, state and local officials had tightened laws regarding prostitution and sex-for-money businesses so much that there were no longer brothels operating in the city, leaving a void where they had long existed. Men took to the streets to find women whom they could pay for sex, and hotels, vehicles, and even alleys became the new venues for these services.

Sex workers found that working the streets alone was dangerous and working with a pimp amplified the peril.

This led to the development of a new kind of brothel, one where women no longer lived but came to work for a shift and went home. Properties that housed the businesses could be smaller and less conspicuous than they used to be, but they needed to operate in a way that appeared to be legitimate. Building on the long-used idea that a massage parlor could disguise a brothel led the mid-century entrepreneurs to begin calling their businesses "health clubs" and "saunas." They applied for and received massage and motion picture licenses from the cities they were in and began hiding behind an air of legitimacy. City inspectors were fooled by massage rooms and sauna areas set up in buildings otherwise used for illegal activity. "Movie nights" were advertised as both an invitation and a cover for the pornographic films shown inside the businesses. Inspections were passed, taxes were paid, and soon a thriving sex industry was working again.

■ ■ ■

As was the case in the red-light districts of old, the massage parlors, saunas, and health clubs of the 1960s and 1970s in Saint Paul were predominantly run by women. Men would be property, business, or building owners, but it was women who ran the day-to-day operations, including hiring, firing, and employee relations. From the very beginning of brothels, these women were referred to as "madams."

Merriam-Webster Collegiate Dictionary defines a madam as "the female head of a house of prostitution." While the massage parlors and saunas of the 1970s did not operate identical to the brothels of the past, they certainly provided the same services, and the women who ran them considered themselves to be madams, as well. Many of the Twin Cities sauna operators carried themselves like the madams of old. They wore extravagant clothing and jewelry while traveling in flashy cars. For years, these women did nothing to disguise themselves, carrying out their business in the light of day. After all, it was the cities themselves that had given them license to exist.

■ ■ ■

IN THE FALL OF 1977, word had gotten out that the owner of the Cosmos City Sauna in Saint Paul was looking to sell the business. The tiny building at 606 Rice Street was nothing to look at, but it was already set up and running. This left a golden opportunity for Clarence and Linda to purchase an already operating business. Cosmos City had regular clients, employees, and the infrastructure to be successful—all Linda and Clarence had to do was keep it going.

The inside of the small structure at 606 Rice Street, what was formally a television shop, had been remodeled into a fully functioning sauna. There were four rooms situated in a hallway off of the front entry and a basement that housed a refrigerator, washer and dryer as well as a safe to keep the day's cash. Each of the rooms had a bathtub or shower and one had a truly functioning sauna.

But it was the lobby that was perhaps the most important part of the space. Inside the front door of the building at 606 Rice Street was a small waiting area blocked off from view of the hallway and rooms. There was a window in the wall of the lobby from which a woman working in the back could speak with a customer out front. The door that led behind the lobby wall was locked at all times. From the outside looking in, the Cosmos Sauna looked like a massage parlor or a doctor's office.

Linda didn't have any money to offer in the partnership with Clarence, but he was more than happy to make the investment. The sauna license held by the owner of Cosmos City was set to expire on November 26, 1977, so after transferring the business itself to Clarence, he and the now former owner made application to the city to transfer the license as well. The city council approved the transfer, and Linda began running the sauna shortly thereafter.

As it had been clearly established in the industry, saunas, massage parlors, and health clubs at the time were offering services other than those specifically advertised. One such service at the Cosmos City Sauna was the screening of adult movies. In order to keep movies in the now-named Cosmos Sauna, Linda applied to the City of Saint Paul and was granted a motion picture license on May 3, 1977. She, too, was now tied to the business, and she and Clarence were running the show.

WHITE — CITY CLERK
PINK — FINANCE
CANARY — DEPARTMENT
BLUE — MAYOR

CITY OF SAINT PAUL

Council File NO. 268965

Council Resolution

Presented By ____ LICENSE COMMITTEE

Referred To _____ Committee: ___ Date ____

Out of Committee By _____ Date ____

RESOLVED: That Application P 13921 for the transfer of Sauna License No. 9954, expiring November 26, 1977, issued to Cosmos City Corporation at 606 Rice Street with President and sole stockholder, be and the same is hereby transferred to Cosmos City Corporation at the same address with Clarence President and sole stockholder.

COUNCILMEN			Requested by Department of:
Yeas	Nays		
Butler		**6** In Favor	
Hozza			
Hunt		**0** Against	By ____
Levine			
Roedler			
Sylvester			Form Approved by City Attorney
Tedesco		APR 26 1977	
Adopted by Council: Date ____			By ____
Certified Passed by Council Secretary			
By ____			Approved by Mayor for Submission to Council
Approved by Mayor: Date **APR 28 1977**			
By ____			By ____
PUBLISHED MAY 7 1977			

Application to transfer Sauna License. City of Saint Paul, Council Archives.

They didn't make many changes at the Cosmos Sauna when they first took it over. Linda brought in a few new pieces of furniture for the lounge area and replaced the shower curtains. New paint was put on the walls, but no structural changes were made. At the time they purchased the Cosmos, there were eight women employed by the previous owner. Slowly, Linda worked to change out the staff so that she had women she could trust working there rather than women who seemed to dislike her.

Clarence was hands off, a silent partner, leaving Linda to the management and operations. For her, it was an opportunity to be her own boss. The money she made at the Cosmos Sauna would be her money, and she didn't have to pay any of her earnings to anyone. She was using what she learned while working in the other saunas to run her own business, and she had dreams of being very successful.

Linda had become a madam. She was no longer turning tricks; tricks were turning for her. Succeeding in this business made her happy, it excited her, and made her want more. And, as the City of Saint Paul was beginning to crack down on sex-for-money businesses, Linda was working on new plans of her own.

606 Rice Street in Saint Paul, April, 2021.

CHAPTER 8

ONE OF LINDA SPENCER'S first acts as madam at the Cosmos Sauna was to increase the "house take" for all services. In order for sauna businesses to make a profit from the provision of sexual services, a system had been developed years earlier, which Linda had learned through her own work experience. Each sauna location had a set price that an employee would pay to "the house" for the services she provided. When Linda started working at Lee Lenore's, the house took $15 per service. This meant that if Linda could talk a man into paying for the highest-cost services, she would make the most money. By the time she was running the Cosmos, Linda had learned that men were willing to pay significantly more, and so she believed she, too, could make more money in the "take."

To get behind the locked door at the Cosmos Sauna, it would cost a man a minimum of $15, which was the cost of a massage and a movie. The services were listed on a board from which a patron could select an amount of time he would like to spend inside the sauna. To a knowing customer, the longer the time, the more in-depth the sexual act. To the unaware, these simply appeared to be length of massage or time inside of the sauna.

Once inside, customers would have the opportunity to purchase additional services, ranging from erotic touching, all the way to sexual intercourse. It was in the negotiation of these services that Linda and her employees made their money. While there was room for negotiation on the part of her workers, Linda would receive a set price for any service provided in her business.

For every sex act performed at the Cosmos Sauna, $25 would be deposited in the safe to be taken by "the house." On average, in 1977 it cost a john $60 to have intercourse with a woman working at the Cosmos. While different women had slightly different costs and terms, this was the general premise on which they all worked, bringing home slightly more than half of the total take.

To track this, Linda used a system similar to those at the other saunas where she had worked. When a customer came into the Cosmos Sauna, a female employee would greet him at the front window and ask what service he would like. Then she would fill out a customer slip. The slip was much like a restaurant receipt that had carbon copies in layers glued together. Each slip listed the customer's first name and last initial, the name of the employee providing the service, and a code to indicate the service to be provided. Prior to going into a room with a customer, the employee was required to separate the top layer of the slip and place it on a spindle on the front desk.

After each service, employees were required to take the second layer of the slip along with $25 and place it in an envelope with her name on it. At the end of each shift, the women were to deposit their filled envelope in the safe in the basement for pickup by Linda or Clarence. If during a session a john added to or requested additional services, Linda required the women to leave the room and fill out an additional slip. Linda ran a tight ship, as she knew some of the games played by sauna employees.

In an all-cash business, it can be difficult to keep tabs on transactions, so for Linda this was her full-time job. Without exception, at the end of every day, the safe was emptied and receipts reconciled. Linda's best defense against being ripped off was to be on the premises at all times but this was not always possible. At the Cosmos Sauna, Linda installed an alarm bell on the front door to track when people entered and exited. This helped her monitor the comings and goings when she wasn't watching, but still there were times when her employees would sell additional services for which they did not pay the house.

This customer receipt system was a key element in not only tracking money but also protecting the women from harm. At any time, Linda was able to go to the spindle at the desk to find out who was in what room and what was going on inside. If the service written on the receipt was to take thirty minutes and Linda found that a woman had been in the room for longer, she would knock.

Linda had a three-knock rule in her business. If after three knocks no one opened the door, Linda or her manager would walk in. There were a few possible things that would typically occur when Linda opened an unanswered door. One, she would find a john begging a woman to give him more for his money. Two, she would find a woman engaged in a service she had not recorded and was therefore stealing from her, or third and most unlikely was that a woman was being hurt by a john. This was not typical, but from time to time it did happen.

Another change Linda made as an owner of the Cosmos was to implement a customer card system. This would help her workers avoid being tricked by undercover cops and, by extension, help her to stay out of trouble. Each customer of the Cosmos Sauna had a card that contained his first name, last initial, and date of birth. When a man came in for the first time, he was asked a series of questions to get his information, as well as to ascertain if he was law enforcement. Linda had learned from women she worked with that making a customer specifically ask for a service tended to help weed out potential cops. So, if a woman was with a customer who did not already have a card on file at the Cosmos Sauna, she was coy with him.

"Never tell them what you will do. Ask what they want," suggested Linda. Once a customer passed this test, his information was written on a card, and he would not have to provide his personal information again. The women at the Cosmos Sauna also used the cards to make notes for themselves and to each other. Customer cards could be found with comments like, "takes forever to finish," or "likes to be tickled." These little notes helped the women make better tips or avoid situations they were not prepared to handle.

From time to time a customer would come to the Cosmos Sauna legitimately looking for a massage. When this happened Linda always struggled to get her staff to take the customer. For them, it wasn't worth the time. For Linda, it was an opportunity. She wanted the women to treat these customers well and try to convince them to purchase additional services while walking the fine line of not getting caught by an undercover cop.

■ ■ ■

LINDA HAD BEEN RUNNING the Cosmos Sauna for less than six months when she began feeling the pressure from the City of Saint Paul. On April 15, 1977, undercover officers from the Saint Paul Police Department entered the Cosmos Sauna and were offered sexual acts in exchange for money. On that evening, two arrests were made, one for engaging in prostitution and one for massage without a license. Six months later, on October 13, 1977, it happened again.

Now, the City of Saint Paul had the ammunition needed to begin coming after Linda Spencer and the Cosmos Sauna. On January 4, 1978, the city council held a public hearing to discuss the revocation of the sauna and motion picture theater licenses held by Linda and Clarence for the Cosmos Sauna. It was not immediately clear what the reason was, but ultimately during the meeting, the council decided to indefinitely hold on the matter. While the council members may have decided to rest on the issue, other city officials and law enforcement did not.

This was when Linda made the decision to join the Saint Paul Association of Sauna Owners. She knew a number of the members from her time working at Lee Lenore's and the Civic Center Sauna, and she wanted the benefit of being a part of the team they had assembled. The association would connect Linda with lawyers to help her in battles like the one the city had initiated as well as provide support in other areas of her business.

With assistance from the association, Linda developed a hiring system for her business. In some cases the hire was easy: a woman Linda herself had once worked with or one she knew. But some women were coming to Linda from a sauna that had closed or who had been fired from a previous job. Linda and the other madams in the association provided both references and warnings to each other about certain women. If a woman had been trouble while working at Lee Lenore's, it was likely she would be a problem for Linda too. If she had a fight with some of the women at one location but was otherwise a valuable employee, she would be worth the risk.

Some women required full interview and vetting. Linda did all of her own hiring for many years. Most interviews were conducted in a hotel bar not far from Rice Street. Linda had a number of items on which the women were evaluated. Appearance was an important part of the job: Did the woman look young or old, was she large or small breasted, blond, brunette, or redheaded? All of these factors were relevant. If Linda had a lot of blond women working at a particular time, she would need redheads and brunettes on her roster for johns who preferred them.

Linda also evaluated a woman's demeanor. How she carried herself was an important factor in determining if a woman would be successful. If a woman was too shy, she wouldn't be able to bring in regulars. If she was too aggressive, she may be a turnoff to men.

Experience was another important part of hiring. If a woman was experienced, it would mean she may come with her own list of regulars. This was a valuable commodity, whereas an inexperienced or first-time worker may not work out at all or end up getting in trouble with police.

CHAPTER 9

DURING THIS TIME OF change for Linda, while she was learning to run the Cosmos Sauna, keep it safe from prosecution by the City of Saint Paul, and make it successful, her personal life began to grow complicated. One day while she was working at Cosmos, a john walked in the door. She was growing accustomed to ignoring them now that she was the boss, but at first glance, she recognized him. Kenny was back. She'd been in touch with him and even visited him in prison on occasion, but she had not told him about Cosmos or Clarence.

Needless to say, Linda was surprised to see Kenny, and he was shocked to see her. She hadn't expected to see him again and certainly not at the Cosmos. Kenny was there for a service but ended up visiting with Linda instead.

Because he had just been released from prison, Kenny needed a job to keep his probation officer happy. Linda was willing to help Kenny by giving him a job doing maintenance work at the building. There were things that needed repair, and Kenny would be cheap labor. Kenny also had nowhere to live when he got out of prison, but Linda was not in a position to help him. She was still living at the house on Clarence's farm, and she was afraid that if he knew about Kenny, Clarence might take the business from her.

Clarence was a kind man who never asked for anything from Linda. It seemed like he simply enjoyed her company. While they were technically partners in the business, Clarence never took a dime.

■ ■ ■

IN THE EARLY MORNING hours of September 28, 1978, Linda was at the Cosmos Sauna, picking up the day's cash, when someone kicked in the back door. Startled by the intrusion, she called the police, and she also called Kenny, who was staying nearby at the Saint Paul Hotel, to come repair the door. Linda spoke with the responding officers, who located and arrested an intoxicated man near the sauna who they believed had kicked in the door. When the police finished their work, and the door was repaired,

Linda, Kenny, and the two women who had been working left the sauna for the night.

A little less than two hours later, police in the area were informed that an individual driving by the Cosmos Sauna had noticed flames near the back door and called the fire department. By the time firefighters arrived, the fire had burned through the now boarded-up back door, and they were forced to make entry through the front of the building. Based on their investigation, police and fire personnel concluded that the fire had been started with gasoline in the rear entryway. Flames ripped through the back area of the sauna, burning the carpet, paneled walls, and some furniture.

The case was taken on by the arson office in the Saint Paul Police Department. A detective spoke with Linda and the women who had been working that evening, along with a few other individuals. From what he gathered, the detective reported that the man who had been arrested for kicking in the door of the Cosmos Sauna had been in jail at the time of the fire. He was ruled out as the arsonist.

Two other individuals had come in contact with the man prior to his arrest and reported that he had been upset with the women who ran the Cosmos Sauna and said that he had been "rolled." These men were furious with the business owner, telling police the place was a rip-off and the people who worked there were crooks. Despite their harsh statements, each of these individuals denied having anything to do with the fire. Without an eyewitness or an admission of guilt, the case proved difficult to solve. After a few weeks of investigating and coming up with no evidence or suspects, the Saint Paul arson detective closed the file.

■ ■ ■

THE ARSON INVESTIGATION DID little to keep Linda Spencer and her sauna off the radar of the Saint Paul city officials. In early summer 1979, it seemed they were beginning to revisit the push to get the business shut down. Late in the evening of June 1, 1979, an undercover officer again entered the Cosmos Sauna. The officer later typed up his notes from the evening, giving a play-by-play narrative of the events of the night.

At approximately 8:15 p.m., the officer entered the Cosmos Sauna and was greeted by a woman who identified herself as Diane*. The officer chose to purchase a $15 massage and movie and handed Diane a $20 bill. She showed him to a dressing room, where he undressed, and then to the sauna and shower room.

Diane returned after his shower and handed the officer his $5 of change and turned on a projector. While she gave him a lotion massage, Diane asked if he had been to any other saunas. The officer indicated that yes, he had been to the Penthouse Sauna, but that they did not give massages there anymore.

The officer inquired of Diane about an "exchange

massage," and she was quick to say it was not on the list of services. The officer asked if she offered it, and she said she didn't know, "you could be a cop." He told her he was not a cop and the reason she didn't recognize him was because he had never been to the Cosmos Sauna before.

The conversation continued with the officer asking Diane how the massage would work. "I massage you in certain places?" he said. Diane again wanted to know how she could be sure he was not a cop, to which the officer told her she could search him if she wanted. Going further, Diane asked what the officer wanted. Claiming to be embarrassed, he didn't tell her.

"You have to tell me," Diane said.

Finally, the officer replied, "I want some sex."

The two began bartering. The officer asked Diane what he could get for $40. "That's under a lay," she told him.

"A blow job?" he asked. "How much is a lay?"

"You name the price."

"Fifty."

"Can you go sixty?" Diane asked.

"For a lay? Okay," the officer said, taking $60 out of his wallet. Diane took the money and left the room, presumably to fill out another customer receipt. As soon as she reentered the room, she was arrested for engaging in prostitution.

Five days later, a letter was mailed to Linda Spencer, informing her that a hearing was to be held on June 27 at City Hall. A license inspector would recommend the revocation of the sauna and motion picture theater licenses for the Cosmos Sauna. This recommendation was based on the very recent arrest of Diane, as well as two previous instances of prostitution at the business.

Linda appeared before the city council on June 27, 1979, to fight. Despite being advised in the letter she had a right to bring an attorney to represent her, she went alone. The city council gave Linda another chance to hire a lawyer and moved the hearing to a later date, but when the council reconvened on July 11, no one came to represent Cosmos Sauna or the licenses, not even Linda. And so, in a vote of four in favor, the Saint Paul City Council revoked the sauna and motion picture theater licenses for the Cosmos Sauna at 606 Rice Street.

The revocations did not deter Linda. She continued to run her business at 606 Rice Street. Other sauna owners were also under the microscope of the City and facing revocations. For their part, the owners and madams began getting creative with their marketing and advertising. Rather than offering saunas, baths, and showers, they offered massages. Others completely renamed or rebranded their businesses. Because it no longer had a sauna license, the Cosmos Sauna simply became the Cosmos Health Club, and continued operating as usual.

CHAPTER 10

Business was booming at the little building on Rice Street. Linda was settling into the role of madam and making the money she always dreamed she would. She was also enjoying the freedom of being able to come and go from the business as she pleased, and not being obligated to a scheduled shift meant she had her evenings free to go out with friends.

Linda's drug use increased during this time. With more money in her pocket, she was able to indulge more frequently. Aside from cocaine, she had also found her way to amphetamines and heroin. While cocaine was still her drug of choice, she found easy access to amphetamines through friends working at other saunas. Just up the street from Lee Lenore's Sauna was a building that housed a variety of medical practices. One doctor in particular had found a brisk business in prescribing amphetamines to women in their twenties and thirties. The doctor did not examine the women; he simply required them to expose their breasts, and he would write a prescription. For Linda, and many other people during this time, it had never been easier to get drugs.

While Linda enjoyed the quiet comfort of her home on Clarence's farm, she sometimes craved the hustle and bustle of the city. Because she kept much of her life a secret from Clarence, she often stayed away from home when she was partying. Linda started frequenting the Saint Paul bars during this time. She could leave the Cosmos Sauna in the evening and go to a bar or club to meet up with friends and then stop by the sauna on her way home to collect the daily receipts at the end of the night.

It was one such evening when Linda was out with her friends in Saint Paul that she met a man she couldn't take her eyes off of. Tom Beier sat in the bar, wearing overalls and drinking a beer. Linda was drawn to his long brown hair and dark brown eyes. When he stood, she saw he wasn't as tall as the other men Linda had dated, but she was attracted to his quiet confidence.

By this time, Kenneth was long gone. Linda had enjoyed

spending time with him and even considered marrying him, but ultimately, she wasn't ready to settle down. Since they had split, Linda had not found anyone she was interested in romantically. It had always been hard for Linda to be intimate; the feelings she had about sex seemed to block her heart, leaving her with an inability to fully connect with any man. But with Tom she felt different.

They started out dating casually. She didn't tell Tom right away that she was a madam. This had become something men were overly interested in when they were around Linda. She wasn't initially ready to invite Tom into all aspects of her life. Linda guarded her secret in the beginning because she felt so differently than she had for the other men in her life. While she told herself she was protecting her business, Linda knew that in many ways she was protecting herself instead.

She knew she was starting to have real feelings for Tom when she was working one night at the Cosmos. Linda was down in the basement doing laundry while thinking about how she could keep the business with Clarence but also get more serious with Tom. She worried that Clarence would leave the partnership or kick her out if she was openly seeing another man. Linda looked up the staircase that led to the upper level. She thought for just a moment about how easy it would be to tie some string across the stairs that would trip Clarence when he came to pick up receipts. It was a fleeting thought, and Linda felt guilty about it, but she knew two things for sure. One, she was going to have a problem with Clarence if he found out she had a boyfriend, and two, she was falling in love with Tom.

■ ■ ■

IT WAS THE SUMMER of 1980 when Linda found out she was pregnant. This had not been part of her plan, but when she told Tom about the baby, he was thrilled. Suddenly, Linda could see her future, not just with Tom, but with children and a home of their own. Tom was good to Linda; he took care of her and supported her. Now that he knew about the business, he was helpful there too. His work in construction made him a great help in keeping the building in good condition, and Linda was impressed by the way he never paid much attention to the women working or showed interest in the services they offered.

Tom's attitude toward the business was contrary to how other men in Linda's life acted around the sauna. Previous boyfriends found their way into rooms with the women or took an interest in the money. Business owners of other saunas were notorious for taking advantage of having sex at their disposal. Even the property owner at 606 came in twice a month for a visit to a room.

Tom did not act this way. He spoke with the women. He wasn't rude, but he didn't fawn over them. He talked about the money and how the earnings would help support their family, but he never tried to take what wasn't his.

Tom was respectful of Linda's role in her business; he never acted intimidated or emasculated by her success.

Linda and Tom partied together quite a bit. They both used drugs, but Tom tended to drink more than do drugs, while Linda drank less than she got high. Tom had found easy access to prescription medication that Linda enjoyed, but partying and drugs weren't the only thing they shared. Linda and Tom had fun together. They loved each other, and it was truly a blessing to them both when Linda got pregnant.

Something happened to Linda when she found out she was pregnant—something in her changed. Although she had been using drugs for years, when she learned she was pregnant, without struggle, she was able to walk away from the cocaine and other drugs without ever feeling an urge or craving. Growing a life inside of her brought Linda a peace she had never known.

Without the haze of drugs or the pull of addiction, she felt dissatisfied with the work she did and wanted to stay away from the sauna as much as possible. Particularly after she started showing, Linda didn't enjoy being around the Cosmos at all.

It was also during this time that Clarence became somewhat of a ghost. Linda assumed he recognized her bulging belly and the presence of Tom around the Cosmos as a sign that she had moved on. He slowly stopped coming to the building, and eventually she stopped hearing from him at all.

They never had a true conversation about his role in the business, nor did they terminate their partnership. One day Linda just moved out of the house on Clarence's farm.

Tom was a good man and a supportive partner who started helping out with the business, giving Linda a break while keeping the income to support their coming child. He took on the receipt pickup duties and suggested his sister, who was already working in the sauna, take over some of the management duties. Tom was never comfortable with his sister turning tricks, so it was easier on him when she was managing anyway.

Tom's sister, Kay*, was a cosmetologist who enjoyed practicing her skills on the women working in the sauna. She was always doing hair and makeup and teaching the women how to make themselves over. Kay was an asset to the business for her management and cosmetology skills. Her presence tended to motivate the women to look better, which was always a benefit to Linda.

CHAPTER 11

UNFORTUNATELY FOR LINDA AND Tom, the pregnancy did not put a pause on the pressure from the City of Saint Paul. On October 14, 1980, an undercover vice officer entered the Cosmos Health Club to investigate prostitution. He was greeted through the lobby window by a young woman with shoulder-length brown hair wearing a black halter-top dress. Upon greeting the undercover officer, the woman asked him if he had ever been there before. Answering no, he was shown a list of services, including a $35 supreme, which he asked her to explain. The woman told the officer that a supreme service would include either a whirlpool or body bath and two movies and two massages. The officer paid $35 and was escorted to a room with a tub.

The woman, who later identified herself as Chris*, told the officer to get undressed and get in the tub, saying she would be right back. He did as he was told and was soaking in the tub upon her return. At this point, Chris kneeled down next to the tub and began soaping the officer, washing and rinsing his arms, legs, and chest. When she was finished bathing him, Chris told the officer to get dried off and again she would be right back.

Now, Chris returned to the room with a projector and started an adult movie as she turned out the lights. The officer lay facedown on the table watching the movie, while Chris massaged his back. The two talked while she massaged him. He said that he was recently divorced and lost everything to his wife. When the movie ended, Chris turned on the lights and restarted the process. She started a new movie and began a second back massage.

During the second massage, Chris talked to the officer some more, telling him she was also divorced and had children. She said she had been in this line of work for three years. As the movie came to an end, Chris asked the officer if there was anything else he wanted. He told her that he didn't have much money left but wondered what else he could get. Following the advice Linda had given her, Chris told the officer he had to say what he wanted, and then she would quote him the price.

"How much would a blow job cost?" the officer inquired.

"Fifty," Chris told him.

"What about a lay? How much?"

"Sixty" was her price.

"I can't afford that. I'm going out drinking and gambling after this," the officer said.

"How much you got?" Chris asked.

"Thirty-five, counting the change you owe me from the supreme," he said.

"You can get a nude hand job for $30," Chris told him.

At this point, the officer told her that he would go out gambling and double his money. He really wanted a lay, so he would come back before the end of the night with $60 for her. He got dressed and left the Cosmos.

Once outside, the officer met with his partner to report his findings. The two radioed for a squad and two more officers arrived. The original officer went back inside and asked for Chris again.

This time the woman at the window hesitated. She must have sensed something wasn't right. The officer identified himself just as two uniformed officers were entering the building and Chris was coming out from the locked hallway. She was immediately informed that she was under arrest for engaging in prostitution.

As Chris was arrested, one of the assisting officers noticed there were two licenses hanging on the wall in the lobby—each one expired. Although the officer was not aware that these licenses had been revoked prior to their expiration, he confiscated them, and they were put into evidence at the Saint Paul Police Department.

■ ■ ■

THE CITY OF SAINT PAUL seemed to be reigniting its pursuit of the saunas and massage parlors. Busts were happening more frequently, and more convictions were being handed down. Part of being a member of the Saint Paul Association of Sauna Owners was being a good steward of knowledge. If one location was busted, the madam or her employees would call to alert the others. They worked as a team to avoid prosecution.

When a woman was arrested for engaging in prostitution inside a sauna or health club, she was most often transported to the jail. As vice teams were formed and investigators assigned, the officers were looking not only to arrest and charge women and men for engaging in prostitution, they were also looking to gather information about the businesses. Arresting a woman or john also gave an opportunity to speak with them during transport or upon booking to attempt to collect intelligence about what went on inside.

For the madams, this was problematic. If a worker was given enough bait, she might start talking. If she was offered a deal, there was always a possibility she would flip and give away evidence leading to search warrants or worse.

When an arrest happened at a Saint Paul sauna, wheels immediately started turning. Attorneys were called, bail money was gathered, and efforts were made to get anyone arrested out of jail as soon as possible.

At the Cosmos Sauna, Tom was the bondsman. His name appeared on many rosters releasing women charged on crimes of prostitution. Linda also sought legal representation for the business and its employees. Having a law firm on retainer made it easy to call anytime, day or night, for assistance getting one of her workers out of jail.

Linda used the lawyers on the frontside process with the women as well. While she took care of finding, interviewing, and hiring candidates for work at the Cosmos, she had the lawyers run checks to verify age and work status. For Linda, it was critical to never hire someone who was underage. It was one thing to look young; it was quite another to be an actual child. That was a line she would never knowingly cross. Using the lawyers to ensure compliance was a safety measure for her and for the women she hired.

■ ■ ■

JUST BEFORE MIDNIGHT ON November 26, 1980, Saint Paul Vice entered the Cosmos Health Club once again. This time the officer was greeted at the front door of the building and immediately asked what he would like. He informed the woman at the door that he would like a waterbed massage plus two movies for a total of $20.

He was shown to a room, where he undressed and was led to the sauna shower room down the hall. The officer took a sauna and shower and returned.

In the room, the same woman he met at the door came in to start the movie and massage. With the projector showing *Dr. Feelgood*, the woman began massaging the officer. She asked him if he had ever been to a health club before. He told her he had been to a place called "Paris" a year earlier. With confirmation that he knew what to expect, the woman began listing services she could provide.

According to her, a hand job would cost $10, oral sex was $40, and a lay would be $60. The officer told her that all he wanted was to "get laid," but that he didn't have enough cash on him to pay her. He would need to go out to his car for more cash. Asking for collateral, she took the officer's driver's license, along with the $38 he had in his wallet. He could have his driver's license back when she got her money.

The woman excused herself and came back into the room and undressed. She lay down on the waterbed and reached out to the officer with an already unwrapped condom. It was with that, the officer identified himself and placed the woman under arrest. He escorted her to the rear of the building to get dressed while advising her of her Miranda rights.

As the woman dressed, the officer asked another employee present if he could use the phone. She said no. While they argued over the phone, the arrested woman managed to run down the hallway and straight out the front door. Dressed in leopard skin from head to toe, the woman took a right and started running north on Rice Street. Soon, a second vice officer was chasing her, yelling for her to stop. The woman was apprehended again and taken back into the building. After a search of her purse revealed two black capsules, commonly known as Blackjacks, and identified by law enforcement as a type of speed, she was taken to the jail to be booked.

The vice officer returned to the police station to determine what charges the woman would face. His first call was to the county attorney, who suggested the case would be better suited for the City because it had been two and a half years since the woman's last conviction, making the charge a misdemeanor. The city attorney suggested two charges, one for engaging in prostitution and one for massage without a license. She also suggested bail be set at $200. Two days later, when the officer went to the jail to present the charges to the woman, he learned she had already been bailed out. An attorney representing the woman had contacted the county attorney, who had set bail at $750. A court date was set for a few days later.

CHAPTER 12

ON MARCH 31, 1981, Linda gave birth to her first daughter. Life was good. Linda and Tom had moved into a nice, small townhome in Saint Paul, not too far from the Cosmos Health Club. The business was running smoothly, and with Kay as the manager, they didn't need to be at the building nearly as much as they had before. For the time being, the City of Saint Paul seemed to be keeping a low profile when it came to the saunas, so things were quiet. The new parents had time to admire their new baby girl, spend time with family, and enjoy all that they had.

Linda loved nursing her baby because she was able

to maintain her sobriety during this time. She knew the life-giving substance her body fed her daughter would be poisoned if she used drugs. Her baby was too important to her to risk. Linda embraced motherhood during that first year, enjoying every moment she could at home and avoiding going to the Cosmos as much as possible.

During this time, Linda learned the importance of being able to separate her mind and her life from the business that supported her. She knew, perhaps deep down, that it was the atmosphere at the Cosmos that made her want drugs the most. Drugs helped her to hide from the feelings she had about the women who worked for her, they helped her to push away her fears of prosecution and being caught, and most importantly, the drugs helped her to keep going. At home with her baby, Linda could be herself. She didn't need to hide her feelings or be afraid that someone was coming to get her. Motherhood felt safe and calm in a way that Linda had craved for so long. Becoming a mother gave Linda all of the things she'd missed out on as a child herself.

Loving and taking care of her baby girl was the biggest responsibility of Linda's life. She threw herself into motherhood in a way that allowed her to grow away from her business almost entirely. She enjoyed the ability to separate from the work, but she also knew the business was essential to her ability to provide for her family in the way she had always wanted—in a way that no one had done for her. If she wanted to give her daughter all the things she never had, she would need to continue to make money.

Time away from the chaos of the business combined with a sober mind left Linda thinking about ways to expand their earning potential. With the City of Saint Paul quiet, she felt comfortable considering the idea of opening a second sauna. Other owners and madams around the Twin Cities were running multiple locations, and Linda knew with her experience, she could successfully do the same.

■ ■ ■

IN THE FALL OF 1982, when Linda found out she was pregnant with their second child, she and Tom started looking for a bigger home and talking about buying a building for a second sauna in Saint Paul.

Even as her maternal feelings made Linda dislike the career she had fallen into, she made the decision to continue on. She understood the financial benefit to running a sauna and grew comfortable with the realization that adding a second location would be a major benefit to her family. As she focused on plans to expand her business, she developed an indifference to the deep-seated guilt she felt for her work and pressed on with a renewed determination to succeed financially.

Linda wanted desperately to move out of the city. She longed for the safety and quiet of a suburban life. As her daughter grew and her stomach expanded, she continued to wish for a life different than the one she had grown up in.

Linda knew she wanted more for her children than

what she had been given. She made a promise to herself: she would do everything she could to give her children more than she'd ever had, and she'd be a better mother than the one she'd known. Providing her children a safe, clean, and comfortable home was so important to Linda. She had lived a cold and chaotic childhood—one she couldn't stand to think of her own children having to live. She would give her children structure in their days, family dinners, and the kind of comfort she had only dreamed about when she was a child. She would give them material things, too—all of the things she never got to have. Her children would have everything they wanted and more than they would ever need.

A nice home on a quiet street in a suburban neighborhood would be the first step in giving her children the life she had always wanted. As the couple searched, they were met with resistance along the way. In one first-ring suburb of Saint Paul, as Tom and Linda stood in the front yard of a beautiful home, they were approached by a man driving on the street. The man was angry as he approached the couple who were admiring the home they dreamed of purchasing. "We don't want your kind here," the man said.

Linda was taken aback. What did he mean? Why would this complete stranger say something like that to her and the father of her children? They hadn't done anything but walk through the home and begin visualizing themselves living there and raising their family. As she studied his face she realized he was a john, a regular at the Cosmos.

Outside of the city, people did not talk about the things that went on in the storefront saunas and health clubs of Saint Paul. Men feared being recognized or, worse yet, outed by a sex worker or madam. Linda worked in a business that was meant to be kept secret and when the man recognized her, he feared the worst. She realized then that living in the suburbs would mean living a life kept secret. She could be both a madam and a mother, but no one could know that was the case.

Linda and Tom did not buy that house they had fallen in love with, and continued searching for a home where they could be not only safe but comfortable. They set their sights on the city of Cottage Grove. It was a moderately sized suburb of Saint Paul, close enough to the city that they could quickly get to the business if needed and far enough away to provide solace from the world where they worked.

▪ ▪ ▪

EMILY JEAN WAS BORN on July 15, 1983, to the open arms of Linda, Tom, and her loving big sister. For Linda, it was another miracle. A second baby girl meant continued sobriety and a welcome reprieve from working in the sauna. Now, they were living in the suburbs just had she had always planned. While Tom focused on building a second location, Linda worked from home, calling into the Cosmos for updates and sending Tom to pick up receipts on his way home in the evenings. She could balance the books at night after her babies went to bed and managed to keep things running from afar.

Linda knew this couldn't last forever. Eventually, when they were running two locations, she would need to start going to Saint Paul regularly to manage the business. While she fought hard against the anxiety that was building inside, she enjoyed the quiet comfort and controlled chaos of motherhood.

CHAPTER 13

THE MINNESOTA STATE CAPITOL building has stood above downtown Saint Paul for over a century. Usually, it is a beautiful building, long and grand, with stairs leading to its front entry. It is a place that holds the history of our past and the hope of our future.

As it sits on this day, the Capitol building looks different. It no longer appears a welcoming place to bring your hope or change. Today, the Capitol is surrounded by blockades. Fences so tall that if a person tried to climb them, they would certainly be caught before making it to the other side. Barricades have been erected to keep out violence and protect not only those who work inside the building's walls, but also the structure itself. These temporary walls are meant to keep out—but in reality, they also serve to keep in. Capitol staff and insiders are not free to come and go as they please. They are monitored, watched, and tracked for their safety and the safety of those around them.

Decades ago, no fences flanked the Minnesota State Capitol building. Lawmakers, staff, and visitors were free to come and go as they pleased. There was no checkpoint at the parking entrance, no one monitoring the ins and outs of the people who visited the building daily. Also nonexistent in the 1980s and early 1990s in Saint Paul were GPS tracking or thirty-second news cycles constantly updating on the whereabouts of anyone, especially not those in Saint Paul.

The Cosmos Health Club was situated just far enough from the Minnesota State Capitol that the people inside could not see who entered and exited the sauna but close enough that it could be visited quickly during a lunch-break. Linda recognized the patrons of her business as politicians, judges, and lawyers, all of whom worked at the nearby Capitol and state court buildings. Suited men often entered the lobby after discretely tucking their cars away on the streets behind the building. These men were powerful. They dressed the part, and the money they threw around when they came in solidified their status. Linda grew to realize there was a certain type of women these men often asked for, and so she changed her schedules to suit them.

The best, most polished, and most beautiful women worked the lunch hour at the Cosmos Health Club. Linda was leveraging the location of her building, and it was paying off.

The lunch-hour business was steady enough in the health club that Linda recognized opening a second location would give her an even greater ability to capitalize on the niche market she was serving. If these men were willing to leave their podiums, offices, and benches to pay for sex at the tiny little building up the road, they would certainly be willing to do so if she built a more upscale and posh location nearby.

As luck would have it, there was a building not too far from 606 Rice Street that was coming up for sale. Just half a mile up the road from the Cosmos Health Club was a beautiful property on the corner of Rice and Atwater. Originally built as a butcher shop and grocery store, the building had a residence upstairs where the owner would traditionally reside. Although they were setting up a wonderful home in the suburbs, Linda knew the upstairs apartment would be a useful place to have for late nights and solace from the world they would build in the storefront below. It would also serve as an office for their growing enterprise.

Linda and Tom talked a lot about expanding their business. This would be a big step for them in a lot of ways. While they had unintentionally taken over ownership of the Cosmos Health Club, they were not the true business or property owners. Clarence still owned the business, although he had, for all intents and purposes, walked away. Buying and converting a new building would solidify their place as owners in the industry, as well as increase their culpability in any criminal cases. But Linda knew this business, and she had proven to herself and to others that she was a capable and profitable entrepreneur.

Linda and Tom signed a contract for deed for the building at 843 Rice Street less than two weeks before Emily was born. The contract allowed the couple to make payments to the property owner until eventually paying off the purchase, rather than taking out a mortgage from the bank. Through this deal, they would be able to purchase their new home in the suburbs while also taking ownership of a commercial property in the city.

Tom started work immediately, converting the old grocery store to a sauna and massage parlor. This was Linda's opportunity to start from the ground up, building a sauna to her own specifications, using all she had learned in her career thus far. She wanted this site to have more working rooms as well as draw in higher-paying customers than those down the street.

■ ■ ■

REPUTATION AND NAME RECOGNITION were important pieces of running a successful sauna business in the 1980s. Having regular johns increased revenues, and one of the best ways to keep johns coming in was to gain a reputation for privacy and discretion. Linda was well known in the business as discrete. Her workers didn't talk, and she never exploited the wealthy or powerful men who came to her sauna.

In order to build a second business, Linda and Tom opted to take the name of the sauna at 606 Rice Street up the road to the new building. The first location was renamed and rebranded as the Como Rice Health Club, and the building at 843 Rice Street became known as the Cosmos Sauna. This would help her keep her current customers, while allowing her to continue to build a larger client list.

The new Cosmos Sauna had six individual massage rooms, each containing a bathtub or shower, along with a massage bed and sink. The rooms were otherwise stark, with only white sheets and towels, massage lotion, and powder. The front entry was built out like other saunas with a false wall obstructing the view from passersby. The basement in the new building was larger than at 606 Rice Street but was similarly situated with washer, dryer and a safe to hold the day's cash.

Linda's goal was to make the new location more upscale than the first. The exterior of the building was already an upgrade from the little white shack that housed the Como Rice. The Cosmos Sauna was formal and sturdy. Its brick façade gave it a mature appearance and its corner entrance gave it a uniqueness that stood out among the other buildings in the area.

The furnishings were all new and much nicer than down the street, a large customer restroom was installed, and shiny black and white tile lined the floors of the hallways. Linda wanted to hire only the best women, attracting high-paying johns as regulars. While things were running smoothly at Como Rice, Linda focused her energy on growing the business at Cosmos.

Along with the fancier location came higher prices, and that meant it was easier to find women to work for her. Linda began hiring and interviewing women of a new caliber. She also found she could attract women from outside of Minnesota with her new higher prices and plush atmosphere. Soon, Linda had women from Las Vegas coming to work for her during the summer months when it was too hot in the desert to bring large volumes of tourists.

The Vegas women were amazing. Beautiful and professional, they brought in a swift business at the Cosmos. There were some men who came to Linda exclusively for these Las Vegas women. But bringing in outsiders had its downside too. Linda's regular workers did not like sharing their space. Linda frequently managed fights between her Minnesota and Las Vegas women. On the upside, the local women worked hard when the Vegas women came, not only to keep up with them but to keep the johns they brought in. Having the women from Las Vegas come every summer became a profitable and longstanding tradition at the Cosmos Sauna.

It didn't take long for the Cosmos Sauna to gain the reputation of a high-class venue where men could come and enjoy not only sexual pleasure but feel confident their identities would not be revealed. Linda and her employees held tight to the names of professional athletes who frequented the sauna, bringing with them mountains of cocaine and other drugs. The better these men treated the women with big tips and free drugs, the more assured they would feel that their privacy would be protected.

843 Rice Street, St. Paul, April, 2021.

CHAPTER 14

OUTSIDE OF SAINT PAUL, Linda was working on building something else—a family. The suburban home she and Tom purchased was now blushing pink with little girls, and as they grew, so did the need to separate her professional life from motherhood. Linda didn't want her peers in the suburban community to know that she was a madam. While she wasn't necessarily ashamed of what she did, she knew others would judge her career choices.

Linda hadn't been used to hiding her work. She may have hidden boyfriends or drugs in the past, but her occupation was something that, until she became a mother, she was proud of. This was a new feeling for Linda. Her family and friends had always known what Linda did for a living. Her mother didn't like it, but she accepted it. Linda's youngest sister worked for her for a short time, as did her brother. But being the suburban mother of two girls made Linda feel the intense need to hide her career. Suddenly, secrecy became paramount.

At the same time she was working to hide her professional life, Linda was also working to separate the person she was at work from the mother she wanted to be at home. As a madam, Linda needed to be strict, fearless, and hard, but as a mother, she wanted to be warm, loving, and happy. It would not be easy to live between two worlds separated so sharply, but Linda was determined to make it work.

In order to solidify the fortress of home life in the suburbs, Linda felt it was important that she and Tom be married. They had been together for years, had two children, ran a business, and owned a home, but they had never taken the step to legalize their union.

The two were wed during a small ceremony at the courthouse in Saint Paul on a Thursday in May of 1986. They did not have a party or a reception. Linda didn't want the fuss. She was in love with Tom and happy to finally call him her husband.

Linda worked hard compartmentalizing her personal and professional lives. She made friends with the neighbors, who believed she and Tom owned a painting company.

The ruse was easy. Tom worked in construction and painting before he met Linda and still drove a truck with construction materials attached. He still wore the coveralls he wore when they met, so he truly looked the part. When asked, Linda would tell neighbors, other mothers, or teachers that she "did the books" at her husband's business.

When her daughters started school, Linda made sure to always put them on the bus in the morning or pick them up in the afternoons. She went to the YMCA to work out in the mornings and got breakfast at the local coffee shop. She wanted to be seen among the other mothers in her world.

Because she owned the business and employed managers to handle some of the daily activity, Linda was able to schedule much of her work around her daughters' needs. While they were at school, Linda would make her way to Saint Paul to check in on the saunas. When they went to bed at night, she could reconcile receipts and prepare schedules for her employees. For a while, this worked well for Linda. She kept a low profile in the saunas, and things ran smoothly. While it wasn't easy to cede control, Linda realized it was a necessity if she was going to manage being a mother and a madam simultaneously.

Although it wasn't simple, the saunas were lucrative for Linda and Tom. The couple was making more than enough money, some years taking home $200,000 or more. They lived comfortably in their suburban home, and as the business grew, they were able to buy things like a boat so they could spend time as a family on the weekends and vacations from Mexico to Disney World. They lived a wonderful life and never wanted for anything. For the time being, it appeared Linda had succeeded in giving her daughters a life opposite of the one she grew up in.

It was never far from Linda's mind, though, what could happen if they didn't have the saunas anymore. She knew the City of Saint Paul was always looking for ways to shut down the industry, and she feared that almost constantly. She could have gotten out of the business and turned to other work to sustain her family, but Linda knew she could never make the kind of income she did at the saunas, and no other career would guarantee her the lifestyle she wanted for her children.

While Tom talked often of other businesses they could start, Linda always resisted. At one time he looked into opening an ice cream shop in Saint Paul, but the profit margins were so small that the couple knew this would not sustain them. Other business ideas came and went, but in the end, they both knew the one they had would be hard to beat financially.

CHAPTER 15

ON THE SURFACE, THE life of a madam appeared glamorous, but behind the scenes, running a sex-for-money business was not only difficult but dangerous. Linda was physically small in stature, but when she was at work, her presence was immense. Almost daily there were situations that required a strong hand. Whether it was an unruly john or a misguided pimp, Linda often found herself engaged in conflict.

It wasn't only outside forces acting against Linda and her business; she also had to deal with internal conflict and employee problems. A near constant conflict existed between madams and their employees regarding money. The simple fact that services took place behind closed doors made it easy for women to shortchange the house. In order to prevent this kind of theft, Linda and other madams needed to have a close eye on what was happening in their businesses at all times. This was hard for Linda because she spent time away from the buildings. When she was there, she could keep tabs on how long a woman was in a room with a john and be sure the proper receipts were filled out, but when she was gone, the employees were left to their own devices.

To manage this, Linda became a force. Early on, she made it known that rule violations would be punished with fines. She made frequent phone calls to check in and would often say she was on her way to the sauna when she had no plans to be there. Linda never wished that her employees feared her; she simply wanted them to respect her enough to be honest in their dealings. Because she could not be there all the time, Linda was forced to find ways to regulate her staff from afar. Instilling a sense of fear was in many ways the only option Linda had. Even before she had children, it was impossible for Linda to be at work every minute the doors were open, but particularly once she became a mother, she wanted too much to be away from the properties and home with her kids.

Linda never truly knew what she would find when she arrived at her saunas each day. Anxiety built as she made her way from the car toward the door. Endless possibilities danced in her mind while she turned the knob and let herself in. On a quiet day, she walked down the hallway among closed doors hearing the muffled sounds of men and women talking or the slapping sound of skin on skin. To Linda, these were the good days.

On a bad day, Linda would walk in to find her business in chaos. Girls fighting, laundry and garbage left out, or an unruly customer causing problems for her staff. These were the times when Linda would get angry. She screamed and cursed until everyone fell into line. Linda was mean when she was angry because she knew she could be easily over-powered by someone bigger than her. While she trembled inside for fear of her own safety, outwardly, Linda roared.

The woman Linda was at work was far different than the one she was at home. It was out of both fear and necessity that she developed two vastly different personas. While Linda the madam and Linda the mother were one and the same, in her daily life, there was no room for these women to peacefully coexist.

◼ ◼ ◼

IT TOOK APPROXIMATELY TWENTY-FIVE minutes for Linda to get to Rice Street from her house in the suburbs. But it wasn't the act of driving that Linda focused on when she commuted. In that time, she was forced to transform herself, not physically, but mentally, to prepare for what was to come. As she drove north toward Saint Paul, alongside the Mighty Mississippi River, Linda would become strong, commanding, and fearless. Thoughts of her daughters fell slowly from her mind as she focused on what would meet her when she got to the sauna. Linda summoned anger from deep within as she drove. As the car gained speed, Linda gained animosity. And as she drew closer to the city, she turned off the mother she'd left in the suburbs, releasing a madam ready to take on anything that came her way.

When Linda turned back south to go home after spending time at the saunas, she would soften. The woman who stood inside the buildings on Rice Street, collecting money for sex, yelling at employees, and fighting off crooks, would slowly find her way back to a sweet, caring mother, ready to hold hands and play with her little girls. The way home, guided by the muddy waters, became a time to transform once again, shifting her thoughts from profits and pimps to diapers and dinner.

It was during the late-night drives home from Saint Paul when Linda's mind wandered the most. The quiet darkness in her car allowed her the time and space to think about all the things she kept at bay in the daylight. While she drove alone, Linda thought about the life she was giving her daughters. She tried so hard to be more of a mother than the one she'd had. She fought tirelessly to be there for her girls, even when it made things more difficult for her, but was she doing enough? Her greatest fear was that her daughters would grow up to be like her. That they would somehow see the things she did and find their way to a life of drugs and sex.

Linda was living two lives so dichotomous they required great strength to navigate. A soft, caring mother would be eaten alive by the women working for her in the saunas. In contrast, the tough, powerful madam successfully commanding respect in Saint Paul would have been a cold and unloving mother, unable to comfort or guide her children. Volleying between two personas took calculation and effort that Linda hadn't been prepared for when she had her children. She learned to confine her transformations to her travel time and hide the toll it took from the people on both ends.

Eventually the duality of her life grew too much for Linda, and she found herself turning to old habits to get by. A line of cocaine in her minivan while she drove to Saint Paul helped Linda fortify herself for what was to come. Another on her way home gave her the push she needed to make dinner, help with homework, and keep the house clean. She found the high of cocaine eased her mind and blurred the fear and worry she carried with her constantly.

She'd meant to start out slowly, to only use the cocaine when she absolutely needed it, but Linda fell fast into the downward spiral of addiction. Cocaine was plentiful in Linda's business. Many of her employees used cocaine, and a lot of her johns provided it. All she had to do was ask. The more cocaine she used, the faster Linda went, and the faster she went, the more money she made. Blinded by drugs, Linda felt fearless and confident. She thought less about the bad things she was doing, and the guilt of being a mother and a madam felt lighter.

But Linda knew she could only go on like this for so long. Her daughters were no longer infants. Soon they would realize their mother wasn't right, and that scared her more than anything. In the middle of the 1980s, Linda decided to give herself a chance, and she checked into a treatment facility in Saint Paul. It would be a thirty-day program, during which Linda would live in the hospital.

Under ideal circumstances, Linda would have been leaving her children and business in the capable hands of her husband, but by this time, Linda wasn't the only one in the marriage who had turned to a substance for comfort. Tom had always struggled with drinking, and this time was no different. While he was supportive of Linda's decision to go to rehab, he was not helpful in maintaining the business while she was away. He had never gone to rehab himself and seemed to have little empathy for her needs during her time there.

At family visits with Linda at the treatment facility, while she was to be spending time with her daughters, Tom discussed problems at the saunas. Instead of reflecting on the things that were important to her and reasons to be sober, Linda spent time in her hospital room making calls to the saunas and conducting business. She worked on schedules, reconciled books, and even mediated disagreements between her staff. She wanted so much to get clean and stay clean, but even while she was in treatment, Linda was consumed by work.

CHAPTER 16

CONSTANT STRESS AT WORK isn't easy for anyone. Add to that the constant investigation and prosecution by a city as determined to shut you down as Saint Paul, and it is not surprising that Linda and Tom self-medicated for so many years.

Throughout the mid-1980s, the city continued to work its way through the saunas and health clubs, convicting both patrons and employees whenever possible. It was no longer a secret what happened inside the storefront saunas and health clubs. There were no exceptions—in the eyes of the city, all of the businesses were prostitution fronts.

On the afternoon of April 30, 1986, an undercover officer entered the Como Rice Health Club. He was greeted at the window by a woman named Tanya*. The officer looked at the list of services behind the woman and requested the $20 lingerie massage that was listed on the board. Tanya led the officer down the hallway to a room where he could undress and showed him where the shower was.

After showering and returning to the room, the officer was joined by Tanya, who began massaging him. While she was giving him the massage, Tanya began asking questions of the officer.

"What are you into?" she inquired.

"Running and lifting weights," he responded.

"No, I mean what are you into with women?"

"Everything, but do you have any suggestions?"

Tanya told the officer that a "French" or a lay would cost $60, or the cost for both was $90. She went on to explain that "everything," including a "69," would cost $100. The officer immediately identified himself and put Tanya under arrest.

Once at the jail, Tanya was charged with engaging in prostitution, bail was set at $500, and she was booked. While she awaited bail, an officer came to speak with her. She was read her rights and asked to sign a waiver. Tanya refused to speak, giving away no additional information.

■ ■ ■

Months later, on December 16, 1986, at 9:00 p.m., Saint Paul vice officers simultaneously entered the Como Rice Health Club and the Cosmos Sauna. At 843 Rice Street, the undercover officer was met at the front door by a blond-haired woman who identified herself as Kristin*. She asked the officer what he was interested in, and he said, "a massage."

Kristin also asked the officer why he had chosen the Cosmos, and he showed her a copy of the *Metropolitan Forum* that had an advertisement for the Cosmos Sauna. He told her he had just been to the Belmont Club and the Faust Theatre and had bought a copy of the adult entertainment guide. Kristin then explained the services and price list to the officer, who chose the basic massage for $25.

"Are you sure? That sounds really boring," Kristin said as she opened the door. She directed the officer to room number two, where he could get undressed, and then to the shower down the hall.

It had always been custom in the storefront saunas and health clubs of Saint Paul for men to bathe prior to receiving any services, especially sexual ones. Women who worked in these businesses preferred the men to be clean and free from any smells they might bring from the outside. Often, the women used the time while a john showered to change into lingerie or fill out any necessary paperwork.

The officer returned to room two after taking a shower and was met by Kristin, who was now wearing a silver leotard. She began massaging him with baby oil and then asked if he would massage her. The officer rubbed her back and told her that he was interested in something more than a massage.

"Like what?" Kristin asked.

"Like maybe a blow job," the officer said.

"How do I know you're not a cop?"

"If I was a cop, I wouldn't arrest you anyway," the officer told her.

"A blow job is gonna cost you twenty bucks more," Kristin said.

"Okay," the officer said.

Kristin left the room again and returned shortly thereafter. She took the officer's money and tucked it into the drawer next to the bed and began putting a condom on him. Just then, the phone rang in the hallway, and someone else inside the sauna called out to Kristin.

She left the room one last time and came back and asked the officer if he had ever been to the Speakeasy Sauna. He said no.

"So you have your ID?" Kristin asked the officer.

"As a matter of fact, I do," he said, now handing her his police identification. "You are under arrest for engaging in prostitution."

The officer asked Kristin where she had put the money he had given her when he first arrived, and she showed him to the couch in the lobby. Under the cushion were two

$20 bills. Kristin was transported to jail and charged with engaging in prostitution, and bail was set at $500.

Down the street at 606 Rice Street, the interaction had been quicker. The vice officer walked into the Como Rice Health Club and was greeted by a woman named Amy*. He asked for the $25 massage that was on the board, but Amy told him no. Then the officer negotiated with her to have a $40 massage.

Amy showed the officer to a room, where he took a shower and sauna, after which he was escorted to another room. Once in that room, Amy came in and rubbed his back for a moment and then asked him to turn over. He asked her when she would take off her clothes. Amy told him that would cost additional money and asked him what he wanted.

The officer told Amy that he wanted oral sex, but that he only had $27 left. She told him that would be fine, and she left the room. When she came back into the room, Amy was naked and began rubbing the officer's body while taking out a condom. The officer then identified himself and arrested Amy for engaging in prostitution. After being charged and booked, her bail was set at $500.

Six months later, the officer who arrested Kristin at 843 Rice Street was called on to talk with a woman who had some questions about the case. The woman had paperwork from the court, along with a form Kristin had signed at the jail on the night she was arrested. She explained she had found the paperwork while cleaning her daughter's bedroom. The officer showed her Kristin's mugshot, and the woman identified her as her 16-year-old daughter. Kristin had used a stolen ID to get a job at the Cosmos Sauna. And she had given that same ID to the police officer on the night she was arrested.

Because Kristin had used a stolen ID to get her job and with the police, Linda was not charged for employing the minor in her sauna. This incident could have had tremendous consequences. It was proof for Linda that no matter how hard she tried, no matter how many lawyers she used, sometimes things would slip through the cracks. She would continue to act vigilantly in her hiring process and proceed with caution as always.

CHAPTER 17

ON OCTOBER 25, 1987, the Minnesota Twins beat the Saint Louis Cardinals in game seven of the World Series. Four of the seven games in the series had been played in Minneapolis, bringing thousands of out-of-town visitors to the metropolitan area. There were parties and events all over the Twin Cities, which, in turn, brought increased law enforcement presence and patrols.

Police investigators were turned into drug and alcohol enforcement, while also taking a special interest in prostitution in the hotels and bars in the cities. Because storefront saunas did not have liquor licenses, it seemed as if many of the businesses were left alone during this time. While madams anticipated an increase in undercover busts, they never saw one. Their businesses enjoyed a major uptick during this time, but they seemed to fly under the radar in terms of prosecution.

But, when the celebrations ended and the winter set in, the Saint Paul vice units once again turned their resources toward the saunas. In early 1988, undercover sting operations started again, and now, investigators were becoming successful in getting search warrants signed for storefront saunas.

■ ■ ■

ON FEBRUARY 1, 1988, undercover vice officers entered the Como Rice Health Club at 4:00 p.m. Inside the front door in the small lobby hung an orange sign that said, "Welcome to Como Rice." Underneath the greeting was a list of services and prices. The "deluxe session number one" was listed at $40, with prices increasing incrementally to number four at $85.

A female opened the small window and asked the officer his name. She introduced herself as Renee* and asked what service he would like. The officer selected number two for $60 and was let through the locked door.

Renee led the officer to a room with a bed and television and told him to undress and go across the hall to take a shower. When he returned to the room after showering, pornography was playing on the television. He waited for Renee to return.

"Are you a cop?" Renee asked when she came back.

"No," he told her. And she left the room, saying she would be right back.

"Are you sure you're not a cop?" she said when she returned again. She began applying powder to the officer's body using a feather duster. While she did this, Renee said, "I'm just paranoid. I don't want to go to jail. I have three kids, and they would die if I got arrested."

The officer stayed quiet.

"Aw hell, I might as well tell you—you paid for a blow job with my clothes on, and you have to wear a rubber."

"What could I get for the $75 number three on that sign?" he asked her.

"For $75 you could get a straight lay," Renee told him. As soon as she finished her sentence, she was arrested.

There were two other women on shift that night at Como Rice. One was told to leave, and the other was asked to stay on the premises while it was searched. While the officers searched the building, the phone rang constantly. The remaining employee was instructed to answer the phone. When she did, she was told by the caller that "all of the saunas are being busted."

Vice officers asked the employee questions about the operations and the sauna. She explained the customer receipt system and told the officers that for each service, $25 was deposited in a safe in the basement. When she was asked who the owners or managers of Como Rice were, she told the officers it was Tom and Linda but that she did not know either of them.

The phone rang again, but this time an officer answered. It was Linda, who had been calling to check in on business for the evening. She refused to give her last name to the officer but said she would send a manager to secure the building. Twenty minutes later, Tom showed up, identified himself as the manager of Como Rice and told the officers that Linda was his wife. He declined to answer any further questions.

A number of items were confiscated from the Como Rice Health Club after a Ramsey County judge signed a warrant in the middle of the night. Officers took customer cards and receipts from the front area of the sauna. They went to the basement and used a lock cutter to open the safe, taking money, envelopes, and additional customer cards. Three pornographic movies, a feather duster, and condoms were taken from rooms, and the orange sign was removed from the lobby wall.

Half a mile up Rice Street, a similar scene was unfolding. As an undercover officer entered the Cosmos Sauna, he was greeted by a woman named Lori* and promptly asked if he had been there before. He told her he had not and was directed to a sign with a price list. The officer decided on a 40-minute session for $60, along with a whirlpool soak for an extra $10.

Search warrant dated February 1, 1988. Courtesy of St. Paul Police Department.

Lori showed the officer to a room with a whirlpool tub and bed and started the water. She told him to go down the hall and shower. The officer went to take a shower and returned to the room and entered the tub. When Lori came back, she was wearing a two-piece lace lingerie outfit. She lay on the bed and began chatting with the officer.

"Are you gonna spend the whole time in the tub or what?" Lori asked. The officer got out of the tub and she motioned for him to sit on the bed next to her.

"What now?" he asked.

"Well, we can start by me massaging you, or you can massage me."

"That sounds good to me," he said.

"You can massage me first," Lori said, lying back on the bed. The officer began rubbing Lori's stomach and near her breasts, but she grabbed his hand and moved it lower. "Do my legs and stuff," she said as she put his hands between her legs. The officer continued on, rubbing Lori in her genital area, and she said, "I know what feels better than your fingers."

The officer looked down toward his penis and said, "I'm ready."

"No, I don't know you well enough yet for that," Lori said.

"Well, then what?" he asked.

Lori answered by wagging her tongue at the officer, indicating oral sex.

He said, "I'm not sure of that. You know … safe sex and stuff."

"I'm safe. I can guarantee you that," Lori said.

"I'm still not too sure of that."

Lori got up and left the room.

When she came back, she had powder and a feather duster. She powdered the officer's body and then told him his 40 minutes were up. Once he was dressed and back in the lobby area, the officer arrested Lori.

Just like they were doing down the street at Como Rice Health Club, officers awaited the signing of a warrant. Once they received word, they began a search. Officers cut open the basement safe and confiscated cash, receipts, checks, and customer cards. They also confiscated a vibrator, employee schedules, customer card files, pornographic movies, and the services sign from the front lobby. Officers found a phone number posted on the bulletin board labeled "management." They called the number, and Tom returned their call, letting them know he would be there soon to secure the building.

About three weeks after the Saint Paul Police had taken custody of the day's earnings at both of Linda's saunas, they received a notice from the IRS that Linda owed some money. In total, the government was looking to collect over $20,000 from Linda, and they wanted to start with the money in the evidence room at the police station. When the agent went to the police department, he collected all of the cash that had been seized on the night of the searches.

So, when Linda's lawyer called to request the return of the money and other items seized in the search, he was informed that the IRS had taken all the cash they collected.

Linda had always relied on Tom to take care of the business taxes. She did not know he had been shirking this responsibility and was furious to learn the development. Now, she had to contend with not only local law enforcement and city officials, but the IRS. Any lens through which the storefront saunas could be viewed simply magnified their blemishes and created more opportunity to shut them down.

CHAPTER 18

Secrets and lies at work came with potentially cata-strophic consequences, but the ones at home were no less significant. Hiding her profession and drug use was not easy for Linda. The older her daughters got, the more it weighed on her. She was in a constant state of worry that someone would find out, that she would ruin her girls' lives, or worse yet—that she would embarrass them.

Linda and Tom had developed a good rhythm in run-ning the business, balancing work and family, but this only worked when they were both sober. When one or both of them were using, they lost control.

Maintaining control was essential to the success of their business and their family. Linda needed to be able to rely on Tom to do things like taxes without oversight, while she focused on day-to-day management of the kids and the business.

Linda and Tom knew the importance of their sobriety, and they tried on multiple occasions to get clean together. When the girls were young, they went with their parents to AA meetings and events. Linda quietly hoped that her little girls would absorb the importance of sobriety and never fall victim to addiction themselves. Sometimes their work paid off and Linda and Tom would have a few weeks or months when they were both clean and sober, but most often, one of them would relapse, and that would send the other back into a spiral.

Problems arose frequently when Linda and Tom tried to hide their using from each other. Linda would learn Tom was drinking again when he was pulled over for drunk driving or when she found a bottle hidden in the house. While drugs seemed to be easier to hide for Linda than drinking was for Tom, she wasn't immune to getting caught.

There were some nights when Linda was home alone with her girls and found herself desperate for a line of coke. This was typically when she had been through a period of sobriety and a stressful event would happen. On more than one occasion, Linda packed up her daughters in the minivan late at night and drove to a parking lot in Saint

Paul to meet her dealer. With the girls in their jammies, tucked in their seats, and covered in blankets to stay warm, Linda would head out without anyone knowing. It was only if her oldest daughter squealed on her that Tom would find out. It happened once or twice that her little one would say, "Daddy, Mommy took us to see the man last night." Tom knew instantly what this meant. Linda never used the coke until she was back home and the girls were tucked safely in their beds, but it was still an incredibly dangerous situation that she put herself and her daughters in to get a fix.

Linda and Tom were a happy couple when they were sober. They had fun together and loved being parents. Linda loved Tom so much it broke her heart when they grew away from each other during their times of use. They tried hard to stay together for their daughters and for the business, but ultimately, the combined effects of drugs and alcohol on their marriage proved to be too much. Tom moved out of the family home in 1989 and into the space above the Cosmos Sauna. He moved the office equipment to one end and set up an apartment on the other. Now, this place that Linda worked so hard to hide from their daughters was the very spot they would go to visit their father.

■ ■ ■

BEING A SINGLE MOM in the suburbs and a business owner in the city was difficult for Linda. Balance became something she desperately wanted but struggled to find.

She would take late-night phone calls from women working in the sauna reporting problems she couldn't fix. Whether it was an unruly customer, a pimp, or an undercover bust, she would spend hours on the phone, trying to maintain her stature and presence while miles away from the people she was managing.

While Tom was still helpful in running parts of the business, he was not adept at conflict resolution and often chose not to handle the dramatic episodes that seemed to pop up so frequently. On many occasions, Linda had to drop what she was doing and drive to Saint Paul to tend to situations that Tom preferred to ignore. He was still drinking heavily, and Linda would often hear from her employees that Tom would come downstairs drunk and walk around the sauna.

Linda needed more help at the saunas than Tom was willing or able to offer. She needed someone she could trust to run the business and the money when she was unable to be there. Linda recalled a man she'd met while trying to get sober who had talked about his own conviction for prostitution, and she decided that he might be a good candidate for the job.

When she approached David and asked if he would be interested in helping her run her business, he agreed. David was like Tom in that he was disinterested in the women working inside the sauna. This was so important because it had been Linda's experience that any man who attempted to work for her, whether as security or maintenance, ended up in trouble with the women. Men seemed unable to separate the business from pleasure, and it always caused problems. With David, Linda could trust that he would do the work that needed to be done and save his personal life for home.

Having David manage the business left Linda with more time to deal with the other things going on in her life. She and Tom were having trouble getting along, which made sharing their daughters difficult. They were living apart in a separation but hadn't yet filed for divorce, so there was no official custody arrangement or schedule for parenting time.

CHAPTER 19

DURING THIS TIME OF marital strife, what Linda didn't know was that the City of Saint Paul was once again ramping up its efforts to shut down storefront saunas within the city limits. Arrests became more frequent at both the Como Rice Health Club and the Cosmos Sauna, but now the police had modified their efforts. Previous policies put in place inside the saunas to avoid undercover police and arrests were no longer as effective as they had been. Customer cards and vetting of johns could not stop the new tactics the vice employed.

It had become clear to investigators that sauna owners

and madams had a system in place to protect themselves from information leaks. Women who were arrested in under-cover operations were bailed out almost immediately after they were booked. The faster they were released, the less of a chance they would turn on their employers to save themselves. If the women were confident they would be released, they tended to be less frightened or willing to talk. This made it difficult for investigators to get evidence of the inner workings of the businesses.

Vice cops working undercover were successfully arrest-ing women for engaging in prostitution inside the busi-nesses, but they wanted more. They needed to put pressure on the johns in order to get a better picture of how the saunas operated. Officers started monitoring the outside of the saunas and catching men leaving. Threatening a married man who had just paid for sex proved to be an easy way to get someone talking. Johns didn't hold much back when they were facing arrest or ticketing that would certainly provide their wives with insight into their late-night or lunch-hour whereabouts. If there was a chance to mitigate the damage, the johns would take it.

The pressure was on, not only for Linda, but for all sauna owners. Members of the Association of Saint Paul Sauna Owners gathered frequently in the park to discuss plans for keeping their businesses open. The owners would continue to communicate when a sauna was busted, helping each other avoid prosecution whenever possible, and they would join together to fight any legal action against them.

There was one Saint Paul sauna, however, that did not have representation within the association—The Cosmopolitan—which was owned by the notorious Rebecca Rand and stood alone in its fight. Ms. Rand was a former prostitute herself who owned saunas in both of the Twin Cities and had made a name for herself with the media by speaking out, quite loudly, about her fight to legalize prostitution in the state of Minnesota.

For the quieter owners like Linda Spencer, Rand only served to draw attention to saunas and cause problems. Rand was flamboyant and made no effort to hide who or what she was. While Linda drove around in a minivan, darting between basketball practice with her daughter to picking up receipts at her business, Rand drove a large SUV with the license plate "Madame." While Linda desperately tried to keep her children unaware of the work their mother did, Rand took her daughter to meetings with the mayor and governor in her attempts to persuade them to legalize prostitution. Rand was a media darling giving headline-worthy answers to questions and using the coverage to aid in her fight. Meanwhile, Linda and the other members of the association tried hard to remain quiet and, for the most part, undetected.

Investigations and prosecution against Rand were highly publicized and seemed to pave the way for similar efforts against other sauna businesses in the Twin Cities. Where people had not previously been aware of what went on inside the storefront saunas, health clubs, and massage parlors, now neighbors were noticing things happening and reporting them to police. Suddenly, city council members were receiving complaints about certain properties, and the public pressure was starting to build.

■ ■ ■

NEWLY REFORMED STATE NUISANCE laws became a useful tool in Saint Paul's fight against sex-for-money businesses. Under the new law, a property could be deemed a "nuisance" when there had been a number of prostitution convictions following arrests at a location. The rule required three or more misdemeanor convictions or two or more gross misdemeanor or felony convictions in two years. Once that benchmark was reached, the city could ask the court for permanent injunction and abatement through the filing of a civil lawsuit against the property and business owners tied to the location.

In the storefront sauna industry, like in many non-criminal industries, there were layers of ownership and management within each business. Building owners leased their space to business owners, who employed managers to run the businesses inside. It was often difficult for the police or city officials to determine who owned or ran the businesses that were operating inside of the buildings. Nuisance lawsuits went straight to the heart of the matter by requiring the property owner's involvement in both litigation and remedy. A property deemed a nuisance lost value, and the owners did not want that to happen.

If the City succeeded and an injunction was ordered, it would require the property owner to end the use of the property for prostitution or prostitution-related activity, which would include nearly all of the services offered at storefront saunas. Abatement required a one-year closure of the building and sale of all movable property inside. For the City, this would be the simplest way to close down storefront saunas and rid the neighborhoods of their presence. While publicly fighting against Rebecca Rand and her Cosmopolitan Sauna, Saint Paul began to assail the remaining businesses.

A quick series of incidents and arrests were documented at the Cosmos Sauna at 843 Rice Street beginning in January of 1990. On January 17, an undercover officer was inside the Cosmos when he was offered oral sex for $60. His suspect went on to advise him that he could receive a "straight lay" for $75 or both a "lay and a blow job" for $90. She was arrested.

A few weeks later, two johns were stopped outside of the Cosmos Sauna. Each admitted to paying for sexual encounters—one, oral sex for $60 and the second, a hand job for $45. In the spring, four additional arrests were made for engaging in prostitution. A similar series of arrests and convictions were happening at the Como Rice Health Club, and unbeknownst to Linda, her former employer at Lee Lenore's was being busted regularly as well.

On February 4, 1991, the City of Saint Paul officially filed a public nuisance lawsuit in Ramsey County against Como Rice Health Club, Cosmos Sauna, Lee Lenore's Sauna, and all of the individuals connected with each business or property. This included Linda and Tom, as well as Clarence, who was still the documented business owner at Como Rice. The property and building owners were also included in the lawsuit. In its complaint, the City asked for a permanent injunction prohibiting the use of the premises for prostitution or prostitution-related activities and an abatement order closing each of the buildings for one year.

Nothing was going right for Linda in the early nineties. While she dealt with the pressure of the City of Saint Paul, she was fighting a separate court battle. Tom had filed for divorce, and they were struggling to find middle ground on anything. While they fought against each other for the children and the business, Linda and Tom were forced to fight together against the City.

■ ■ ■

LOCAL ATTORNEY S. MARK VAUGHT had been working with a number of sauna businesses to defend women who were arrested for prostitution. Now, he was hired by the owners and operators to represent them in their battle against the City. Vaught went to work, asking the court to separate the lawsuits into individual actions, organized by location and the related individuals. So many properties had been sued in semi-random groupings, it made sense to individualize the cases. Once that was done, he asked the court to merge them again in a larger group, which would then fight hard against Saint Paul. There was power in numbers as much as there was an advantage to standing alone.

None of the locations, including the Como Rice Health Club or Cosmos Sauna, shut down during this time, despite the City requesting temporary injunctions on many of the properties. The court had not granted the temporary injunctions, so the businesses remained open and operational.

Vaught was prepared to fight hard on behalf of Linda and all of the individuals involved in the case. He developed and presented to the court a complex legal theory based on evidence he had gathered that the City of Saint Paul had orchestrated a "carefully planned effort" to "identify and close certain establishments located within the city."

Vaught contended that the city council, city attorneys, license inspectors, and the Saint Paul Police Department had all been involved in the effort. He went on to present that it was the city attorney who worked to "amass a substantial number of convictions to use in these civil proceedings by literally offering the criminal defendants 'a deal they couldn't refuse.'" He alleged it was all an effort to collect the statutorily defined number of convictions in order to file suit.

Vaught argued that the sauna owners and operators were not given proper notice by the City of Saint Paul to abate the acts that were the subject of the convictions. In short, a property owner was supposed to be informed of convictions at the property and given an opportunity to gain control of the situation prior to a nuisance lawsuit being served. According to Vaught, the City withheld the conviction notices until it was able to get enough evidence to invoke the nuisance statute. It did not give the property owners any opportunity to take action against the businesses in their buildings before the lawsuit was filed.

The final argument Vaught presented stopped just short of accusing the city attorney of prosecutorial misconduct. The argument centered on his theory that the City of Saint Paul was so intent on shutting down saunas that the prosecutors were directed to obtain convictions by any means necessary. This meant that any person arrested in or near the premises of a sauna for any crime involving prostitution was offered a plea deal so good it couldn't be passed. Having defended many individuals charged in these cases, Vaught was well versed with the plea deals and able to draw on his own files for evidence.

In his legal briefs, Vaught included transcripts from many of the plea hearings of those convicted prior to the nuisance suit. On December 3, 1990, a woman was in court for the charge of aiding and abetting the operation of a disorderly house as well as engaging in prostitution. Vaught argued that this woman had been intentionally overcharged and subsequently offered an attractive plea deal, including an expungement, in exchange for her guilty plea. This meant that the woman would, after accepting the guilty plea and staying out of trouble for one year, have no criminal record. In this case, and many of the others cited by Vaught, even the judge seemed perplexed by the significant plea bargain being offered by the prosecution. During the plea hearing, Ramsey County Judge George Peterson asked the attorneys into his chambers for a discussion regarding the deal. After returning to the bench, he asked the prosecutor to not only present the deal but explain its departure from "ordinary policy" for the record. The city attorney made the following statements:

> Currently the City Attorney's Office is focusing on the establishments, the sauna/massage parlors. And as a part of an effort from the City Attorney's Office, we're attempting to get convictions on these locations so that we can utilize the City ordinance on which will attempt to shut down these sauna/massage-type parlors.

> Based upon that policy, Your Honor, we are offering a stay of imposition to workers of the—these establishments. As a way to induce them to plead guilty, we offer a stay of imp. The stay of imp gives us a conviction on these locations which we can proceed, Your Honor, against the locations which

we're actually after and hopefully shut down the locations so there's no place for these actions to occur in the future.

The Saint Paul city attorney who briefed in opposition to Mr. Vaught seemed less than pleased by his arguments. The brief opened with a four-page explanation of "prosecutorial motivation." In this section, the City presented its own argument that none of the defendants prosecuted were injured in any way and that there was no coercion in the "constitutional sense in the plea agreement offers."

Continuing, the brief argued that law enforcement had the right and obligation to develop strategies and policies for enforcement of criminal and civil laws. Finally, the City argued that this kind of plea bargain was available to any and all defendants charged in similar matters, not only those related to the subject saunas.

Vaught shot back with another brief, this time making arguments against the chief prosecutor for the City. He again cited transcripts where assistant county attorneys presented plea bargains to defendants and were questioned by judges as to the City's reason for offering deals that were a departure from the typical practice. Along with the statements from the early December 1990 hearing, Vaught included additional statements for this brief. Quoting an exchange between a different judge and prosecutor than the first case, he laid out the judge's question and prosecutor's response:

The Court: Why do you want to make such a generous offer?

Prosecutor: That was an offer, I understand, my office has made with defendants in matters of this nature. One of the intents was to get convictions on certain establishments so those establishments might be closed down. Therefore, the intent of this action, or actions of this nature, [were] to get a number of convictions at certain establishments.

The chief prosecutor claimed these two assistant county attorneys' statements to the court were "erroneous, albeit undoubtedly not intentionally so." As if laughing out loud on paper, Vaught wrote that his clients submit to the court that the transcripts perhaps "state how things really are and [the chief prosecutor]'s affidavit is a statement how she wished they were." He was not buying the prosecutor's response and didn't believe the judge should either.

Vaught finalized his defense eloquently by presenting an argument that showed his understanding of the process and pieces of the City's case. He agreed that individually many of the City's actions were not problematic. It is not out of the ordinary for police to make arrests and city attorneys to offer bargains. It was, according to Vaught, "the nexus between the deals made with the criminal defendants in furtherance of this action that 'taints' these convictions so that they should not be used as a basis for this civil action."

Vaught never argued that crimes did not occur. He never attempted to discredit police in their undercover work or claim that prostitution was not occurring in the Saint Paul storefront saunas. His argument was based in process. For its part, the City of Saint Paul had not followed the rules in gaining convictions or notifying the business and property owners of said convictions. He argued that the owners had no opportunity to remedy the problems occurring on their premises, and therefore injunctions and abatements were not proper. Point by point, piece by piece, the two sides fought each other on these issues. The opponents met often in courtrooms in Ramsey County, passionately presenting their stance and fighting hard for their side.

CHAPTER 20

MANY PEOPLE DURING THIS time saw the life of a madam as luxurious and simple, thanks to Rebecca Rand and her boisterous dealings. For Linda May Spencer, it was nothing of the sort. Linda had two buildings to run, with dozens of employees and even more problems. In a nearly 24-hour operation, there were hundreds of things to be done each day. For the safety of her employees and the success of her business, Linda was a strict madam.

At the Cosmos and Como Rice saunas, many things were expected of employees. Each woman was required to clean a room after use. All surfaces were to be wiped, sheets and towels removed, and any discarded items were to be put in the garbage and taken out. Linda had a hard rule against food in her buildings. There was to be no eating in public areas or rooms, and if Linda walked in and saw one of the women eating, she would get angry. Cleanliness was an issue for Linda. She required near perfection when it came to sanitation.

Linda learned early in her career that being the boss meant being tough. She cared for her staff and their safety, but she kept boundaries between them. Unlike madams of old, Linda treated the women like employees, rewarding them for hard work and disciplining them when there were problems. At Christmas, the women of the Cosmos and Como Rice saunas were treated to gifts and a company party. The women knew if they worked hard for Linda, she would reward them graciously. She was generous with time off and allowed her employees a flexible schedule when needed.

Because Linda had two locations, she was also able to have a structure that encouraged the women to compete and work hard. She started inexperienced women at the Como Rice Health Club with the promise of promotion to Cosmos when they were ready. She was also able to punish women at Cosmos who did not follow the rules. Being sent to Como Rice after having worked at Cosmos was a demotion, and the women worked hard to avoid it.

Safety of her employees was paramount to Linda. She worked hard to keep pimps away from her business, as they were known for hurting women physically and emotionally. She also kept a close watch on johns coming into her saunas. The majority of men were not there to harm the women, only to find sexual pleasure, but from time to time, incidents occurred.

One critical safety measure put in place in Linda's businesses was related to scheduling. Linda and her managers never scheduled only one employee to work in the building at a time. For the safety of her staff, they were always scheduled in twos. If there was a time when only one woman was needed, a manager would be in the building. But this was not a perfect plan. Sometimes a woman would fail to show up for her shift or someone would be ill and have to leave early.

January 28, 1992 was one such evening. During the previous week when the schedule was written, two women had been scheduled to work that night, Melody* and Denise*. But just a few days before, Denise had been arrested during an undercover bust and she decided to quit her job at the Como Rice Health Club. The manager had been able to replace Denise with a new employee and that woman was scheduled to work with Melody on January 28.

Melody worked most of her shift without issue, although as the evening progressed it became clear that the new girl would not be showing up for her shift. When two men came in together asking for services, she told them that only one could come in, as there was a policy that she could only have one man in the back because she was alone. The man, who called himself Jimmie*, paid Melody $45 to enter the sauna.

When she opened the door, Jimmie and his friend both came through. Not knowing what to do, Melody told the men to go into the bedroom and she would go call another employee to come in for the second man. As she did, her former co-worker Denise came into the sauna to collect her belongings. Melody told Denise what was going on and Denise said she would help her straighten out the situation before she left.

Together Melody and Denise walked into the room where the men were waiting. Both had already showered and were wearing nothing but towels around their waists. Jimmie told Melody that he wanted all four of them to have sex in the same room. Denise spoke up and told the men that it was against policy to have more than two people in the room and that Melody should not have let them in together in the first place. Denise left the room, indicating that she would go find someone else to come in.

"What are you doing?" the man asked Denise as she walked back toward the room she had left.

"I was trying to find someone to come in for you," she replied.

"How 'bout you grab me a pop?" he asked her.

Denise knew this would be a good opportunity to separate the men. She had an uneasy feeling. Melody was in the room with Jimmie but this man in the hallway seemed angry; he refused to tell her his name and yet insisted he would stay and receive sex. She showed him to a separate room and said she would get him a soda.

As she returned to the room, he grabbed tissues from the table and wrapped them around the can. He then laid four $100 bills on the table and said, "I want to freak with you."

Denise declined.

"Come on, girl. You know why I'm here. Freak with me. Suck on me and I'll lick you," he said.

"I don't even work here anymore," Denise said as the man grew angry.

The man waved more $100 bills, fanned out in his hand, saying, "You can have it all if we fuck with no rubber."

Denise shook her head no and watched as the man became agitated. "Fine," she said, "I will blow you, but you have to let me go get a rubber." She moved toward the door.

"Alright," he said quietly. The man opened the door and moved into the door frame, watching Denise as she walked to the lounge to get a condom. He closed the door behind her when she came back in. "Take off your clothes."

Denise stripped down to her bra and underwear and the man pushed her back onto the bed. She handed him the condom and began performing oral sex on him. As she took his penis into her mouth, the man grabbed Denise by her hair and forced himself into her throat, choking her repeatedly.

When he removed his penis from her mouth, Denise was momentarily relieved. But he moved down her body, forcing her legs open and putting his face between her thighs.

"Put your finger in my ass," the man said as he repeatedly forced his tongue in her vagina.

"No," Denise said, "I won't do that."

"Come on. Get freaky with me. Freak with me," the man said.

"No," Denise repeated.

The man then got up on his knees, removed the condom from his penis, and penetrated her mouth again. He pushed and pulled his penis in and out of her mouth for about five minutes until he stopped again and forced himself on top of her, putting his penis into her vagina.

"Please don't hurt me," Denise cried.

"Shut up," he said.

"You can have all of my money, please, just don't hurt me," she cried louder.

The man covered her mouth with his hand. "If you don't shut up, I'm going to take this knife and stab you." He leaned over the side of the bed, putting his hand between the mattress and box spring. When he brought his hand back up, he did not have a knife, but he pulled his penis out of Denise and flipped her over onto her stomach. The man then grabbed her by the hips and lifted Denise up on to her knees, her face still flush with the mattress.

He tried numerous times in this position to anally penetrate her but ultimately did not.

Melody could hear the muffled cries from across the hall. She grew increasingly concerned for the safety of her friend as she finished servicing Jimmie. As soon as she was dressed, she ran out of the room to check on Denise.

As the man grabbed Denise and flipped her over on to her back again, the door opened. Now, Melody and Jimmie were standing in the room while the man was on his knees on top of Denise on the bed. "Jerk him off," Jimmie said to Denise.

She did and very quickly the man ejaculated on Denise's stomach and climbed off the bed.

That's when Jimmie said, "We're FBI, you are going to need to give us ID and all of the cash you have."

"Come on, girl. Where's the money?" the other man said to Denise.

"In my purse, out there," she said, indicating toward the door. The man left the room. When he returned, he was dressed, and he opened Denise's purse and emptied it onto the floor.

Both men began looking through the women's things and taking money. Jimmie asked Melody for the money he had given her. "It's in there," she said, pointing to her purse that he was already holding.

"This ain't it," Jimmie said, looking at a $20 bill he pulled from her wallet.

"Our cash was marked. If you keep it, you are gonna get killed."

"Just kill her," the other man said.

"It's out there," Melody said, pointing in the direction of the desk. She had put $30 in an envelope for the house and left it on the desk when she opened the door for Jimmie.

The men gathered the money they had found in the women's purses, along with the sheets, towels, and pop can, and went running out the back door. The women were relieved that the men were gone but terrified they would return.

Melody heard the phone ringing and ran to answer it. Luckily, it was her boyfriend and she told him they had been robbed and hung up the phone. Minutes later Saint Paul Police arrived at the Como Rice Health Club.

After conducting interviews, line-ups and investigations, police were able to identify one of the two men who had gone to the Como Rice Health Club that evening to rape and rob the women working there. While the man had been brought in on charges for criminal sexual conduct and robbery, he was ultimately allowed to plead guilty to felony simple robbery and served less than a year in jail.

An incident like this was not common but sheds a bright light on a number of issues. First, it is not hard to imagine what could have happened to this woman had she been in a hotel or alley with this man. Although it was not a perfect system, the protections Linda and other madams put in place did help to deter this kind of violent crime. Scheduling two employees at all times was a critical piece of providing security in the saunas.

The two women involved in this incident were told by the men that they were undercover FBI agents. While it seems outrageous to consider this claim true for even a moment, it was not farfetched at the time. By 1992, undercover busts of storefront saunas had become a regular occurrence. Police officers conducting stings entered the businesses requesting services just as these two men did. It was not uncommon for undercover officers to be naked, aroused, even engaged in sexual touching prior to identifying themselves as police.

And finally, in the failure of the justice system to convict this individual for criminal sexual conduct, we see the innate bias against sex workers. Because women willfully engage in sex for money there was and is an assumption in society that she "asked for it." If a woman offered sex, she was somehow responsible for assuming the risk that the customer may harm her. Sex workers then and now continue to struggle with the stigma associated with the trade.

CHAPTER 21

DURING THIS TIME, WHILE the City of Saint Paul pushed hard against them, Linda and Tom remained combative in their divorce proceedings. While Vaught was fighting for the rights of the sauna owners and operators, Linda and Tom were fighting each other to be awarded control and ownership of the business. In June of 1992, in a petition to the court in their divorce case, Linda argued that she was the sole owner and operator of both the Cosmos Sauna and the Como Rice Health Club businesses, and that although Tom had assisted in management and operation of the locations, he was not ever transferred any ownership rights.

Tom responded in an affidavit filed days later. He claimed that it was he, not Linda, who managed the saunas. In sworn testimony, he wrote that he collected receipts, paid the bills, and managed employees. Tom argued that Linda's life with the children in the suburbs prohibited her from being at the businesses. These assertions were interesting, as just a few months prior in a separate sworn statement, Tom had claimed that the two had successfully run the business together for many years.

In his efforts to obtain the businesses, Tom also criticized Linda's personal life. He alleged that her relationship with David had become personal and that the two had set up an additional business inside the existing ones to earn money that would not be accessible to Tom. He accused Linda of being a bad mother and a bad business owner in his court filings. The divorce was becoming more contentious as time went on.

In what was to be the final divorce order, a judge awarded Linda and Tom joint ownership of both of the businesses as well as the building that housed the Cosmos Sauna. Tom would remain living in the upper-level apartment at 843 Rice Street and Linda would continue to run the businesses and her household in the suburbs. Neither Linda nor Tom were satisfied with this decision by the court. They would go on to fight for years in post-divorce proceedings.

■ ■ ■

It was August of 1992 when a Ramsey County judge finally denied the City of Saint Paul's request for injunction and abatement against the Cosmos and Como Rice saunas. This was a relief for Linda, but her attorney was quick to remind her that the fight was not over. Just one week later, the City of Saint Paul filed their appeal with the Minnesota Court of Appeals. Included in the case were Lee Lenore's, The Speakeasy, and the Emporium, all sauna locations within the city.

When the case reached the upper court, there was one simple issue on which the outcome hung: Did the public nuisance law require a separate notice of conviction to be sent to the building owners and other parties after each conviction, or could they be sent in bulk, as had been done by the City of Saint Paul in the outset of the lawsuit?

The City of Saint Paul argued that when the law was constructed, it simply stated that "a notice of a conviction" be sent to building owners and interested parties. On the basis of the letter "a," the district court in Ramsey County had determined that the City was obligated to provide a notice of conviction at the time of each conviction. The sauna owners argued that sending all of the convictions in one notice did not allow time for building owners or parties to remedy the alleged nuisance prior to being sued.

The Minnesota Court of Appeals agreed with the district court and the sauna owners. In their reading, the letter "a" did indeed require a separate notice for each conviction, and therefore the City of Saint Paul had not followed the law. In its opinion filed March 3, 1993, the Minnesota Court of Appeals effectively concluded the nuisance cases against the saunas. In the end, the City of Saint Paul had lost on a technicality.

■ ■ ■

THE CITY OF SAINT PAUL and the sauna owners and operators had become fierce adversaries through the many battles they had endured. It was clear early on that neither side was going to back down. Before the appeal was filed, the City was well on its way to making enough arrests and convictions to file nuisance suits once again.

Things were in full swing for Linda at both of her businesses. She had managers running each location but found herself still working in the buildings more often than not. While her daughters were in school, Linda would drive up to Saint Paul to work. After getting her daughters off the bus and having dinner, Linda would head out again late in the evening, leaving the girls with family or babysitters. Once again, striking the balance between mother and madam was catching up to Linda.

But the money was good and steady coming from the saunas. The Cosmos Sauna was pulling in high-paying johns, and Linda's women were working hard for her. The Las Vegas women had served to not only increase business but also to teach Linda's Minnesota women how to be better.

Now, she had women working hard to stay at Cosmos, rather than getting scheduled to work at Como Rice. This competition was good for business.

Word of mouth was also spreading in the Twin Cities. A john looking for privacy and discretion could count on it at the Cosmos Sauna in Saint Paul. Linda had professional athletes, politicians, doctors, even law enforcement officials coming to her sauna.

For a short period of time, the lawsuit and legal battles even served to keep busts to a minimum at Linda's businesses. The quiet and comfortable feeling went a long way toward increased business, as well. While other saunas in Minneapolis were under a police microscope, the Como Rice and Cosmos were tied up in court but otherwise being left to operate uninterrupted.

■ ■ ■

THE QUIET DIDN'T LAST long. On July 7, 1992, an undercover officer entered the Cosmos Sauna. On that evening, an employee asked the officer to undress her. While she started to place a condom on him, she was arrested. During an interview at the police station, the employee was shown a series of index cards, which she identified as "customer cards," and when asked what the customers were there for, she told the investigator, "sex." Five additional arrests were made for prostitution on that same night at the Cosmos Sauna.

The police were changing their methods. Undercover officers were not always easy to identify, so the sauna owners came together to work on strategies for the women to use in an effort to stop some of the arrests. Keeping the women out of jail and away from interviews with police remained a top priority for the owners. The immediate bailout method wasn't working as well as it had previously, so stopping an arrest before it happened became a new defense mechanism.

Linda began sending her women to classes put on by local lawyers. There, the women were given tips to weed out potential undercover cops. One suggestion given to the women was to require men to specifically ask for what they wanted. A typical john would give a clear answer, while a cop might attempt to get information by questioning what services are offered and how much each would cost. Another strategy for women to use once a man was in the massage room would be to request that he perform a sexual act on her first. The theory was that a police officer would be required to turn down this suggestion. It would take a lot of maneuvering to identify and dismiss a police officer, but if it could be done, it would be a huge benefit to the business.

Rules were changed and policies were updated. A customer card now reflected whether a john had been willing to give a woman oral sex. If he had, he was certainly not a cop. The women were able to pull out the customer card to see this information prior to taking a john into a room.

If the card deemed the john was not a cop, the woman was much more comfortable. If there was no card or the card did not have the correct designation, she would know to be careful.

CHAPTER 22

With Tom still fighting her in family court, a booming business did little to help Linda with her stress. Although Tom was living away from home, she still had to deal with him on a near daily basis, and they were trying to co-parent their daughters, as well.

Tom's drinking had been a problem during their marriage, and it remained so during their divorce. While Linda was doing lines of cocaine, Tom was drinking vodka. Long after he'd moved from the home, Linda's daughters found broken glass in the basement crawlspace. Tom had been drinking and hiding the evidence right under their noses.

Tom's drinking led to more significant incidents than Linda's drug use. Tom was arrested and convicted for drunk driving many times during their relationship. In the early 1980s, he crashed Linda's brand-new Jeep into a utility pole, causing thousands of dollars in damage. Luckily, he was not injured. Tom found himself at many times without a valid driver's license due to drunk-driving charges. He frequently used public transportation or taxis to transport himself and his daughters when they were in his care.

It was Emily's ninth birthday in 1992 when her father decided to take her to spend the day at the zoo. She was in heaven. A whole day with her dad and a celebration just for her! They went to the zoo, and as the day went on, it started to rain. Emily noticed that her dad started acting really silly. He was jumping in puddles and dancing around. At the age of nine, Emily was aware of the possibility that her dad had been drinking, but he was being silly, not mean, so she didn't mind.

When it was time to go, Tom found a taxi to take them home. This was one of those times when Tom's driver's license was suspended due to his drunk driving. Emily rode in the back seat with her dad as they made their way toward his apartment at 843 Rice Street. Emily had been there plenty of times before. She knew this was where her dad lived now.

Tom told Emily he had to run upstairs to get their swimsuits. They were going to go swimming at the YMCA.

Emily stayed in the taxi and waited excitedly for her dad to come back downstairs. After about thirty minutes had gone by, Tom had still not come back to the taxi. Emily was starting to get scared in the backseat of a stranger's car, but she didn't know what to do. She knew she wasn't supposed to be out on the street by herself, and she wasn't allowed inside the downstairs of the apartment building. The driver had gone to the side door that Tom had entered to knock a couple of times, but no one responded.

Finally, someone came out of the back door that Emily recognized. It was Wanda, one of Linda's managers who sometimes looked after Emily and her sister when they were upstairs visiting their dad or when their mom took them to Saint Paul with her. Wanda gave the driver the address for Linda's house, and soon Emily was on her way home.

Linda was waiting outside when Emily arrived. Wanda had called her to tell her what happened, and she paid the taxi driver as soon as he pulled in the driveway. Linda was blind with anger. She had taken risks with her daughters, had them in situations that could have gone bad, but she was always there with them. She was sober when they were awake. She was there. Tom had left Emily with a complete stranger in a vehicle while he went upstairs and passed out from drinking. Anything could have happened.

■ ■ ■

JUST A FEW MONTHS later, a fire was started in a massage room at the Cosmos Sauna. After showing a john to a room, one of Linda's employees smelled smoke. Returning to the room, she saw that the man had started a fire on the mattress. The building was immediately evacuated as the fire raged. Rather than calling the fire department, the women working got into a car and drove down the road to the Como Rice Health Club. Luckily, a neighbor noticed smoke coming from the building at 843 and called 911.

The two-alarm fire caused over twenty-five thousand dollars in damage. Investigators ruled the fire an arson and took to ruling out Tom and Linda as suspects. To clear themselves, both were required to go to the police station for questioning. As Tom filled out a questionnaire in the presence of his attorney, he wrote that he had been out bar hopping at the time of the fire.

The Cosmos building had to be closed and business stopped during the time it took to repair all of the damage. Linda moved the girls working in that location to the Como Rice Health Club and continued taking as many johns as she could get in during the closure, but it did cause a lot of problems for her employees. Shifts were harder to come by and regulars who had grown used to the niceness of the Cosmos felt uncomfortable in the smaller and more rundown building up the road.

CHAPTER 23

POLICE BEGAN TURNING UP the heat on the saunas again at the end of 1993. Now, squad cars were seen sitting near the sauna buildings and uniformed officers were patrolling the streets outside. Along with deterring johns from entering the saunas, the police were speaking with them to obtain information about what was going on inside the buildings. It seemed this time the police wanted to do more than just accumulate convictions; they wanted to shut down the owners and operators, as well.

Word ran quickly through the sauna owners. They were all on the lookout for each other and in near constant contact with lawyers who could help them. Linda received calls on many evenings warning her that busts were coming in her buildings. There were times when Linda would call her locations and tell the managers to close up for the night to avoid possible infiltration by undercover cops.

More than that, though, this time around, the police were watching Linda at home. She often noticed a police car on her block when she came home at night or left in the morning. Linda was bold. She waved to the police officers and carried on as if she were untouchable. She knew she was being watched, and she knew exactly why, but she wasn't going to be intimidated by the police.

What Linda and the other owners were unaware of was that by this time, the Saint Paul Police Department had set up a Special Investigations Unit specifically to deal with the saunas and health clubs in the city. They were aggressively working to rid Saint Paul of prostitution and had planned a series of highly synchronized raids within the city.

⬛ ⬛ ⬛

ON JANUARY 19, 1994, an undercover vice officer entered the Como Rice Health Club at 606 Rice Street. The officer was outfitted with a wire and had $200 in marked $20 bills. Upon entry, the officer observed a man at the front window speaking with a woman who asked him what he would like. The man told her he wanted "half an hour" because he had to get back to work. The man was let in the door and escorted by a second woman down the hallway.

As the officer stepped up to the window, he was met by the same woman. She asked him if he would like to come in, to which he said yes. Behind the woman in the window, the officer could see a board with a list of times and prices, ranging from $60 to $100.

"The last time I was here, I got a blow job," the officer told the woman in the window. "What's a half and half?"

"We do everything here by the hour, honey," she replied, dodging the question in an effort to avoid giving specifics. The officer elected to receive a half and half for $90.

Once the officer passed the payment through the window, he was let in and told to go to the last room on the right. There, he was asked if he wanted to take a shower, to which he said no, and the woman told him to get comfortable and she would be right back. When she returned to the room, the woman was wearing black lace lingerie. As the officer lay down on the bed, the woman took off her clothes and began giving him a massage. After a few minutes, she asked him if he would like to finish the backrub or just "get started."

"I'd like to get started," he told her.

As the woman reached into her purse and pulled out a condom, she explained, "I'll start with a hand job and then ... you don't even know what you're getting, do you?" she asked, recalling the question he'd asked in the lobby.

"No," the officer responded.

"You get a blow job for half and sex for half," she explained.

"I am an officer with the Saint Paul Police Department, and you are under arrest for engaging in prostitution," the officer said.

Law enforcement stationed outside the building, listening on the wire, heard the arrest and prepared to enter. As they secured the scene, the officer asked the woman for her identification and was directed to her purse. He searched the purse and found $80 of the $100 he had given to her for the service. When he asked where the other $20 had gone, she told him she had put it downstairs in the safe.

Down the hall, officers saw a second woman exiting one of the rooms wearing white pants and a black bra. As they went to the room, they found a partially dressed, now terrified man, who told them he would probably be getting divorced now and how stupid it was to do this. He told officers he had been to the Como Rice Health Club on other occasions and usually got a hand job to relieve stress. Officers arrested the man and both women and all three were transported to jail.

With vice officers now inside, they prepared for the second part of their sting operation. First, officers went to the basement to secure evidence. Upon discovering the safe, they forced it open. Inside they found envelopes of money and receipt slips with customer and employee names.

Also inside was a note written to Wanda* asking for time off on January 30.

As the officers continued to search the basement of 606 Rice Street, they found various documents, including certificates of occupancy for the building, employee schedules, and a list of rules for working in the sauna. They also uncovered a card with a list of other saunas and their phone numbers.

After removing evidence and taking the three individuals arrested out of the Como Rice, another team of undercover officers made their way inside. Female officers were now taking over the operation and would pose as employees of the sauna. These officers changed into outfits they had selected with the intent of being mistaken as employees of the suana, including spandex pants, high-heeled shoes, and sweaters. They also gave themselves names for the undercover operation—they would be known for the day as Candi and Cindy.

The phones at Como Rice started ringing as soon as the officers took over. Between the hours of 11:00 a.m. and 4:00 p.m., police estimated about one hundred calls came into the sauna. The calls were made almost exclusively by men, except for calls from Linda and her manager, Wanda, checking in on business. The incoming calls were determined to be customers based on the questions being asked. The officers took calls inquiring about services, the cost for different sexual acts, what women were working, and what the women who were working looked like. They were also asked more specific questions, such as would they spit or swallow semen while giving oral sex, and if they would be willing to take more money to have sex without a condom. For their part, the officers seemed shocked by the nature and volume of the calls.

It was mid-morning when a man came to the door. Candi greeted him, and he asked how many women were working. After learning there was one other woman in the sauna, the man asked if he could see her. When Cindy came to the front, he asked the officers how much it would cost to have sex with both of them and if they would be willing to engage in a sexual act while he watched. They said they would, and he then asked if one of them would perform a dominance act with him. They told him that either of those things would cost extra money, and the man said he would go to a cash machine and come back.

Just before noon, a woman called the sauna and identified herself as Linda. She wanted to know how business was that morning. The officer on the phone told Linda it was slow. Linda said, "Okay, that's not good, but keep bringing them in. We need the money." Just a few minutes later, a man called and identified himself as Tom from Cosmos, also asking how business was that day. The officers gave him the same information.

Throughout the morning, the officers struggled with the phone lines. They believed the cord on the phone was faulty and went in search of a new cord to install. Without a new cord, they had trouble answering calls and keeping calls connected, but they proceeded despite the problem. A short time after the call from Tom, a woman called Como Rice and identified herself as Wanda. She asked how business was and was also informed that it was slow. Wanda asked how many women were working, and she was told there were three.

The front door of the sauna opened at noon and a man came to the window. The officer posing as Cindy greeted him. The man asked if there were any women with "large breasts" working that day, and he was told that Candi would be available in a few minutes.

When the man returned, Candi greeted him, and he selected the thirty-minute, $60 package. Once in a room, the officer said to the man, "Okay, you've been here before. Do you want a blow job for sixty bucks?"

"Yes," the man replied.

"I have to go fill out a ticket," She said. "I'll be right back."

When she came back to the room, the man asked the officer, "How big are you?" She responded with her bra size, and as she spoke, the man reached out his hand and grabbed the officer's left breast. She grabbed his arm, swung it away, and immediately arrested him.

At ten minutes before 1:00 p.m., Linda called again. The officer noted that her tone had changed and now she sounded angry. Not knowing she was speaking to an officer, Linda said, "What the fuck is going on there? You should be busier than that. I'm on my way there. I'm right down the street."

After a brief conversation, officers inside the Como Rice decided to play out the situation. They did not believe that Linda knew they had taken over her business or that anyone had been arrested there earlier. In all the calls they had taken, no one had questioned who they were or seemed to identify that they were speaking with a stranger. Because of the high turnover of women working in saunas, combined with the alternating hours Linda and Wanda worked, neither of them considered the strange voice on the other end of the phone could be law enforcement. Each just assumed it was someone the other had hired.

The officers returned to taking calls and Linda called again. This time she asked how many women were working, but before the officer could answer, the phone cut out. After about ten minutes, the officer was on the phone again and Wanda called, but again the phone line went dead. Now, Linda was on the line again and she was angry.

"What the fuck is going on there? What the fuck are you doing?" Linda screamed. The call-waiting clicked in. Linda told the officer to answer the other line. Wanda was the other caller and said she would hold while the officer spoke to Linda. "What the fuck is going on there this afternoon?" Linda yelled again. "How many are working?"

"Three. Candi, Jenny*, and Cindy," the officer reported to Linda.

"Well, you should have had more than two in!" Linda said. "What the fuck are you doing?"

"There have been more than two. We've had seven."

"Why did you tell me before there were only two?" Linda asked in anger.

The officer tried to backtrack. "When you called, there were two in rooms. We've had seven total and most of them have been full sessions."

"What the hell are you talking about? I've been watching. Two guys went in and one hasn't come out. What the fuck are you up to? If you are fucking around, you are all going to pay me thirty bucks!"

Between the time Linda said she was right down the street and the most recent claim that she was right outside, three additional officers had arrived at Como Rice. They were quickly tucked into a room and out of sight before Linda arrived.

At 1:50 p.m., Linda walked into Como Rice and went right to the desk. "What's going on here? Where is the spindle?"

"Right here," the officer pointed.

"Where the hell are your slips, and where is Jenny?" Linda yelled.

The officers tried to explain to Linda that "Jenny" was in a room and that they had already deposited their slips because they were getting ready to end their shifts. Linda was getting angrier. She wanted to know why, if Jenny was in a room, there was no slip on the spindle. She went to the room where the officers hid and knocked on the door.

"Jenny, where is your slip? It's not on the spindle," she yelled through the door.

Luckily one of the officers in the room was a female and yelled back, "It's somewhere by the couch."

Linda went looking. As she was looking around the couch, the phone rang again. "Como Rice," the officer said into the receiver.

Linda's head whipped around. "Why are you answering the phone like that?" She picked up the phone herself. "Como Rice Cosmos," she said as she answered. "What the fuck is wrong with this?" She held the phone out to the officer, still not recognizing that the two women were not her employees.

They explained they had been having trouble with the phone all day and that they looked for another cord but couldn't find one. Linda said she knew there was another one around somewhere and she would go downstairs to find it. Once Linda went downstairs, the officers went to the massage room to get the others. They knew that when Linda got downstairs, she would find the lock broken on the safe and know that something bad was happening. They all turned as they heard Linda yell, "What the fuck is going on here?"

When she reached the top of the stairs, Linda Spencer was arrested. Before they left the sauna, Linda asked if she could retrieve her checkbook from her purse. She had her lawyer's phone number in her checkbook and would certainly need to call him soon. The officers declined to give Linda any of her belongings and transported her to the police station.

The vice officers stayed inside the sauna, planning for what would be the next phase of their investigation. As they were preparing to leave, there was a knock on the back door. The officer who opened the door was greeted by a woman who looked very surprised to see her. She said she was there to pick up Theresa, and the officer told her Theresa would be done soon and she could come inside to wait. The woman declined. The officer recognized the woman's voice as Wanda, who had called the Como Rice earlier in the day. She advised a second officer who went outside to engage the woman and identify her. Eventually, she admitted that, yes, she was Wanda who had called the sauna twice that morning, and the officer escorted her inside the building. Running a check revealed that Wanda had an outstanding warrant for engaging in prostitution. She was put under arrest immediately.

The arresting officer searched Wanda's purse. Along with her wallet, a mirror, and cosmetics, Wanda had job applications, a schedule for sauna employees, and a book of phone numbers. Once these items were logged into evidence at the police station, they were cross-referenced. Many of the names in the address book were the same as those on the schedule, and some showed up on the applications, as well. Each application had a blank space for "work name." Some of these names also matched those on the schedule. Officers had taken a schedule that hung on a bulletin board at Como Rice, and again, the names matched.

By this time, officers from the Saint Paul Special Investigations Unit had taken into custody two employees, one manager, two johns, and the owner of the Como Rice Health Club. It was time to begin the process of interviewing these individuals to get as much information as they could from each before they were booked and able to bail out.

Linda was the first to be interviewed. She was informed by the investigator that she had been booked for promotion of prostitution and possession of a controlled substance. Linda explained that when she had gone to the basement of Como Rice to look for a phone cord, she had seen some white stuff and a straw sitting on the washing machine. She didn't know exactly what it was, but assumed it was drugs, so she took it and put it in her purse and went upstairs to yell at the women.

"I don't do drugs," Linda told the interviewer.

What she had forgotten, however, was that when she went downstairs that afternoon to look for a phone cord, she had left her purse upstairs by the phone. Police were already in possession of the purse when Linda came upstairs.

They had found a bundle of cocaine and a straw tucked inside her checkbook when they searched it later, and they were using this to charge her with possession.

Trying to cover her tracks and distance herself from the operations at the sauna, Linda told the investigator interviewing her that when she was down in the basement, she had noticed a vodka bottle and a bundle of cards with a rubber band around them. She didn't know what the cards were for, but she had noticed them there and wanted them to know she had seen them. She told them she believed her employees had probably been drinking and using drugs in the basement and they had left these items there.

When asked who owned the building at 606 Rice Street, Linda said it was her, but as the interviewer began asking questions about the history of ownership, Linda lawyered up. She was walking a fine line, and she knew it. At Como Rice, Linda did not own the building and technically she didn't own the business either. At this time, Clarence was still the business owner, although he had never once in all the years taken a dime from her as payment. The building owner leased the space to Como Rice Health Club for about $500 per week, but other than coming to the sauna for services a couple of times each month, he had nothing to do with the business itself. Linda didn't wish to identify the men who gave her the opportunity to have her business. She didn't want to get them into any more trouble than she already had in the past.

Wanda was the next to be questioned. Her story had changed multiple times from her introduction at the door of the sauna. She first told officers she was there to pick up an employee. By 7:30 that night when an investigator entered her holding cell to question her, Wanda said that she was actually at the sauna that day to return her pager and keys.

Wanda had moved to Minnesota from Indiana about ten years prior. She began working at the Cosmos about two years earlier and was transferred down to the Como Rice when a mattress had caught fire in Cosmos and caused too much damage to have customers. During that time, Wanda said, there were so many women working at Como Rice it was hard to make a living. She asserted that she had stopped coming to work, and after a series of part-time jobs, she had landed a job at a bank. Coincidently, she claimed, it had been just the day before that Linda had left a phone message instructing her to return her pager and keys to the sauna as soon as possible and that, unfortunately, had been the reason she was at Como Rice on this day. Wanda went on, telling the interviewer she had just gotten married in December and her new husband had no idea she had ever been a prostitute.

When asked about the owner of the Como Rice, Wanda said she had never met her but knew her name was Linda. She had also heard some of the other women talking about a man who may have been an owner, but she didn't know his name.

Wanda said that Linda would call the saunas all the time and women would tip each other off when they knew she was coming. Sometimes Linda would show up, of course, never when Wanda was there, and she would yell at the women and be very angry if things weren't perfectly clean and tidy. Wanda said that Linda was usually drunk or high when she called in asking about business each day. Wanda would recognize her voice, but again, had never met her.

When questioned about the operation of the sauna, Wanda said she thought it was Linda who emptied the safe nightly. Throughout the day, the women would deposit $30 into the safe for every trick. There was no management at the sauna, according to Wanda. It was up to the women to determine leadership on each shift, and it was usually the women who had been there the longest who would take charge. Wanda didn't make the schedules and didn't know who did.

The investigator knew that Wanda was lying. Based on the items found in her purse and the paperwork collected at the Como Rice, it was clear that Wanda, had a hand in scheduling employees at the sauna. Taking a new approach, Wanda was informed that Linda had been arrested. The interviewer told her they were much more concerned with Linda's promotion of prostitution than they were with Wanda's engaging in it. Wanda held firm. She maintained that she didn't know much about Linda. She knew that Linda had been in the business for many years but didn't have much else to offer. With that, the interview concluded, and Wanda was left in the holding cell to await booking.

While investigators at the station were busy interviewing the arrested, another team of officers was headed to the suburbs to execute a search warrant at Linda's house. Officers arriving at the Spencer home were surprised to find Linda's ten- and twelve-year-old daughters home alone. After a family friend came to pick up the girls, a search was underway.

Many items were confiscated from Linda's home. Among them were keys hidden in a coffee can, a blue plastic file box, and mountains of paperwork. Officers found over fifty slips and envelopes in the trash that matched the ones found in the safe at Como Rice. They also found sauna schedules, job applications, and accounting records in Linda's bedroom. Tax and property records confirmed Linda Spencer was the owner and operator of the Como Rice Sauna as well as the Cosmos Sauna at 843.

One of the officers who was part of the search had been working with the vice teams on investigating saunas for quite some time and was able to provide information in the report that gave explanation and importance to many of the items found at Como Rice and Linda's home. The officer wrote:

> In all of the reports of this investigation, reference is made to tickets, slips, guest check envelopes with

cash amounts, employee[s] names on them, and customer names. Also mentioned is the drop box.

I have worked in the vice unit for a number of years and have done numerous sauna/prostitution investigations. The following is a summary how the money, customers, and employees are kept track of.

When a customer (almost strictly male) comes to the Como Rice, a female will talk to him through a barred opening. There is a list of services on a board that usually lists time and money. The regular customers know each of these sessions are for a particular sex act.

- Number 1, 60 minutes, $90: this is usually a half and half (slang for oral and regular sex).

- Number 2, 50 minutes, $75: this is usually intercourse.

- Number 3, 45 minutes, $60: blow job, slang for oral sex.

- Number 4, 30 minutes, $40 to $50: hand job.

At different saunas/health clubs, the prices may vary slightly, but this system is used in almost all saunas.

After the customer picks a particular service, his money is taken and he [is shown] to a room. He is told to take a shower and she'll be back. The customer is asked his first name, his first initial of his last name, and his DOB. A card is made out on this customer, if he doesn't have one, and he will have to do some sexual act or touching to prove he is not a police officer. The customer will receive what sexual service he paid for and then leave.

The female employee will make out a restaurant-type guest check in duplicate. On the guest check will be the date, time, rm. number (which at time is what session you had), the first name of the customer, first initial of the last name, DOB, and the female's first name. This will be placed in an envelope, and on the outside of the envelope there will be the date, shift the employee works (3–12), cash amount in the envelope (at Como Rice it is usually $30), and the guest check number. The guest check, customer's card, and $30 will go into the envelope and be dropped into a large box with a slot. This lockbox usually has a padlock and is opened up daily. The $30 is a portion of the money the owner receives for her sexual services. The guest check is then placed on a spindle, and at the end of the shift, it can be determined how many customers were in and how much money was taken in. The guest checks are in numerical order, so the people running the operation will know if they are not getting their full amount of money.

This is a general overview of how most sauna/health clubs that are fronts for prostitution are run. There are slight variations and price differences, but on the whole, most are set up this way.

Based on all the evidence collected at the Como Rice Health Club and at her home, Linda Spencer was charged with promotion of prostitution and possession of cocaine. She was transported to the Ramsey County Jail, where she would spend at least one night until bail was set. Unlike most of the inmates at Ramsey County Jail, Linda was given a room to herself. Word had made its way to the jail that Linda was a madam and officers were concerned she would attempt to recruit women during her stay.

Being in jail was not easy for Linda, particularly because she was isolated. She worried about whether the others who had been arrested would be talking to cops. She worried about her daughters being scared and sad when they found out their mom was in jail. She was withdrawing from cocaine and starting to feel ill as she lay alone in her cell. On her second day inside, Tom brought the girls to the jail to visit Linda, but she was so sick and so angry that the visit had not been a relief to her at all.

A few days later, bail was set at $7,500, and Linda was released after Attorney Vaught made arrangements. Linda was free from jail, but felony charges hung over her head. Vaught got to work on a defense immediately. It would be a difficult case. The undercover operation and takeover of the business had netted the police a great deal of evidence against Linda. They had been able to tie her ownership and operations at the sauna and prove she was not only aware but involved with the prostitution occurring inside Como Rice.

Six months later, Vaught presented his defense. He argued in court that all of the evidence collected against Linda should be suppressed and therefore the charges against her dismissed. Vaught claimed that the evidence the police had obtained had been collected through an illegal search, and so the charges against her were not viable. Splitting the sting operation on January 19 at Como Rice Health Club into separate phases helped Vaught argue his point.

According to Vaught, the first phase of the sting was fair and legal. The undercover officers entered the Como Rice to conduct the operation and had cause to do so, based on previous convictions for prostitution at the location. After arresting two women and one man inside the business, officers made a "protective search" of the building, still operating legally. It was in entering the next phase when officers took control of the business and continued to search rooms and secure evidence that things took a turn. Vaught argued that from the time the first set of arrested persons were removed, and the protective search concluded, officers were required to obtain a search warrant. He went on to argue that any evidence collected after the initial search should be suppressed because there were no exigent circumstances giving rise to a warrantless search during the time the officers had control of the Como Rice.

Eliminating evidence collected from the time of officers taking over operations would also eliminate charges against Linda, as it was during this time that she entered the Como Rice, went downstairs, and left her purse; it was also during this time that the police obtained documents linking Linda to the Como Rice Health Club. Vaught argued the search of Linda's home, collection of evidence, and impounding of her vehicle were all illegal search and seizure because the warrant obtained for this action was based on the collection of evidence during the illegal search of Como Rice. Vaught laid out the phases of the operation like dominos, and though the first fell into the second and subsequently the third, the first should have stood alone.

On July 13, 1994, a Ramsey County District Court judge agreed with Vaught. In his memorandum, the judge was careful to point out that "there certainly is indisputable evidence that the club was being operated for the illegal purpose of prostitution," but he went on to explain that the only evidence of Linda's association with the sauna or the illegal activity occurring there was obtained illegally. Ultimately, based on the judge's findings that the second phase of the search had been illegal, the felony charges against Linda were dismissed.

Linda had dodged a bullet. She was free from criminal charges, and for the time being, her business would continue to operate.

While the criminal case played out against her, the City of Saint Paul seemed to be making a two-pronged attack against Linda Spencer and the Como Rice Health Club, adding a civil lawsuit to the mix. A new public nuisance suit had been filed just prior to the commencement of the sting operation and updated once the convictions from the operation had been entered. Vaught fought against this case, as well, alleging that the new convictions obtained through the sting operation were at least in part not viable because, as the judge had decided in criminal court, some of those convictions had been obtained as a result of an illegal search and seizure.

The City of Saint Paul had taken great care in this filing. After having lost a series of suits a few years prior, they were diligent in sending conviction notices, researching property ownership, and keeping suits against individual locations separate. The City had built a strong case against the Como Rice Health Club.

■ ■ ■

THINKING HER CRIMINAL TROUBLES were behind her, Linda was able to once again focus her attention on her business and what she saw as a great injustice in the division of assets in her divorce from Tom. During the previous year, Tom had remarried and spent less of his time with their children and the businesses. He had also been sentenced to thirty days in the workhouse for alcohol-related offenses and attended a thirty-day treatment, leaving Linda to run the businesses alone.

For her part, Linda felt if she was doing all the work, she should be receiving all the profits. Through her attorney, Linda filed a motion requesting a reallocation of the 50/50 split originally assigned by the court for the Como Rice Health Club and Cosmos Sauna. Tom argued through affidavit that Linda had never complained before about the division of proceeds or amount of work. He claimed that during his sixty-day absence, Linda had operated the saunas as if she had been the "sole owner" and had not divided receipts with him. According to this filing, Tom had taken two weeks' worth of receipts for the two buildings and totaled them to find a $15,000 net proceed. Tom alleged Linda was sitting on approximately $9,000 in net proceeds after paying all of her employees.

The judge partially agreed with Linda this time. In an order dated February 13, 1995, specific operating duties were outlined to be carried out by Linda and others by Tom. In the order, Tom was to make all decisions concerning operations in the saunas, including hiring, firing, and scheduling, while Linda would be responsible for all the financial work. The judge went so far as to order Tom and Linda to meet every day at 10:00 a.m. to go through the prior day's receipts. Linda was to collect and divvy, according to the order, all income from the businesses. Tom and Linda would continue to jointly own and operate the saunas.

But, what the judge in the divorce case did not know when he made his decisions on sauna operations was that by this time, the Como Rice Health Club had been shut down.

CHAPTER 24

ON DECEMBER 9, 1994, the City of Saint Paul officially won its civil nuisance suit. A permanent injunction and abatement were ordered at 606 Rice Street. The court found that based on seven convictions between 1992 and 1994, the City had met its burden in proving the Como Rice Health Club was a public nuisance. The judge ordered the closing of the business, a one-year closing of the building in its entirety, and the removal of all property "used in conducting the nuisance." The order was clear: all signage should be removed, and no sauna or other adult activity was to be conducted on the property ever again.

Since it started its fight, Saint Paul had been slowly chipping away at the sex-for-money businesses in the city. First to fall had been Pam's Holiday Lounge in 1991, followed by the Red Carpet Health Club in 1992, which had moved locations after losing its lease to a nuisance complaint and then closed after a second battle was lost. The year 1992 had also seen the closing of the Cosmopolitan Adult Health Club owned by Rebecca Rand when she was sentenced to six months in jail and paid $200,000 in civil penalties. It was nearly two more years before the city was successful in closing the Como Rice Health Club. Linda was lucky that she had avoided criminal prosecution.

The success of the City of Saint Paul in the fight against the businesses seemed to slow after the shutdown of Como Rice. It continued to investigate, setting sights on other businesses, but it also began enlisting the help of the public. Community activists at the time had identified storefront saunas as the biggest blight on the neighborhoods of Saint Paul. In an effort to shut them down, community members organized a protest at the home of an individual who owned the building that housed the Speakeasy Sauna. As luck would have it, the owner of the building was also an employee of the City of Saint Paul in the health and human services department. He succumbed to the pressure of the community, closing the business before the City's nuisance suit was heard in court.

■ ■ ■

WHILE MANY OF THE Saint Paul madams had pulled up stakes, Linda May Spencer had no intention of backing down. She had made a career of this business and, although she had lost a piece of it, she wanted to continue on.

It was during this time that Linda's true business acumen seemed to propel her. Rather than closing down, Linda doubled down. She raised prices at the Cosmos Sauna, hired more workers, and started taking notice of the kinds of services her customers were requesting.

Throughout time, women who worked in saunas were subject to many strange requests from johns. An entrepreneurial woman could use these requests to sneak extra money in her pocket. Once johns became regulars and knew the rules at the sauna, they were good at talking women into what they wanted. While it may have cost a john $60 for oral sex with a thirty-minute session in the room, a woman could be talked into being paid more to do something else for those thirty minutes. More than once, Linda walked in on a woman dripping hot wax on a john or heard spanking sounds as she walked down the hallway. It wasn't that she disallowed these services; she wanted to be paid more money if they were provided.

By the mid-1990s, men had become bolder in their requests, asking women to dominate them, hurt them, even humiliate them. When Linda walked into the Cosmos one day to find a man, whom she knew to be a local judge, crawling down the hallway wearing a diaper and sucking on a pacifier, she knew there was money in these new kinks.

Plans were immediately drawn to convert the basement of the Cosmos sauna into an S&M dungeon. The walls were painted black and Linda began installing apparatus to simulate torture and dominance in different areas of the basement. Linda started collecting whips and chains to be used on customers and allowing her employees to provide these services on request. What had previously been racks with feather boas and lace lingerie slowly began changing over to leather corsets and metal spiked bras. Trends were changing, and Linda was ready to change with them.

She found new employees looking for work as she got the word out that she was building the dungeon. Soon, Linda was interviewing women for the role of dominatrix. These women would come to interviews dressed in leather, carrying suitcases full of their "tools."

CHAPTER 25

LINDA SPENT THE MAJORITY of her life surrounded by sex. She made her career figuring out what pleased men sexually and putting a price tag on it. But for all the time she put into thinking about, facilitating, and earning a living from sex, it was something Linda herself had very little personal interest in. From such a young age, Linda had been taught that there was no pleasure in sex, only fear and pain. Men in her life had let her down since the beginning, leaving her with such revulsion and mistrust in the gender that she rarely encountered a man she would allow into her life.

Tom was an exception and Linda truly loved him. Not long after their divorce, Linda learned that Tom had gone to Las Vegas and married one of the women who worked for her at the Cosmos. That hurt Linda, but as she predicted, the marriage didn't last.

It was when he moved in with another woman years later that Linda felt, once again, the betrayal of a man she'd once trusted. There had been a couple in Linda and Tom's life from nearly the beginning that they spent a lot of time with over the years. Linda had been skeptical of the relationship between Tom and the other man's wife, but Tom always assured her they were only friends. When Linda learned from her daughters that Tom had gotten that woman pregnant, she was devastated. It had never been easy for Linda to give love to a man, and while she never thought that she and Tom would be together again, she had always felt he still loved her, and she'd never truly closed her heart to him. Learning that he was expecting a child with a woman she had once considered a friend was a finality for Linda that she hadn't seen coming. It was a loss of the only love she'd ever really known.

■ ■ ■

WITH THE CLOSING OF the Como Rice Health Club, Linda no longer had Wanda, but David remained the manager, and in many ways her partner, at the Cosmos Sauna. Linda found comfort and companionship with him, and

they were together often. They never formalized or identified their relationship, but at times Linda and David were
intimate. David had stepped into Tom's shoes, both inside
and outside of work. She didn't love him the way she loved
Tom, but she trusted him, and for her, that was a big thing.

At home, Linda's two daughters were older. They were in
high school and, for the most part, becoming independent.
She worried constantly that her daughters would somehow
fall into the lifestyle she had tried so hard to hide from them.
She insisted that they were busy all the time. If they weren't
in sports, they were required to have jobs—she didn't want
them to have downtime that may provide an opportunity
to engage in drugs or other things that might lead them
down the path their mother had taken. She worried about
who their friends were and how they dressed. It stressed her
out when they went to parties or came home late at night.

As her girls grew into women themselves, it became
harder on Linda to see the women working for her doing
the things they did. She tried hard not to engage on a
personal level with her employees. She didn't want to feel
for them or worry about them like she worried about her
daughters. This became a new weight on Linda that she had
to balance in her divided life between madam and mother.

More and more, the only thing Linda could do to get
through each day was to get high. She needed cocaine in
the morning to dull the ache of yesterday's high wearing
off. She needed a line on her way to the city to prepare

her for arriving at work. A bump in the afternoon chased away exhaustion from a late night spent driving home from Saint Paul, and a line before she left in the evening to go home erased the sins of the day before facing her daughters. By nightfall, Linda had been high all day, and allowing a slide would leave her too tired to go back to collect the day's receipts. It was easy to fall into the cycle of existing in a steady state of weakened emotions and heightened efficiency. Linda enjoyed the numbness, as it prevented an onslaught of guilt that she knew was constantly lurking below the surface.

Her increased drug use meant an increase in expenses. She was spending a lot of money buying cocaine at the same time her receipts were down due to the loss of the Como Rice. In response to the need, Linda became an even stricter madam. She began holding mandatory staff meetings at the Cosmos to remind her employees of the rules they were to follow. It became more important than ever to keep up the appearance of legitimacy inside the sauna. Getting busted by undercover operations or shut down for health reasons would be catastrophic.

Linda became hot tempered and short-fused. She had little tolerance for the drama her employees brought to work with them and often came to the Cosmos yelling as she walked through the door. If she walked in to find things out of order, Linda would fly into an angry tirade. If she believed an employee to be stealing from her, the employee would be fired immediately. Linda lost her patience for any kind of rule violation. One evening when she walked in to collect receipts, Linda found one of her employees sitting in the lobby, eating a hamburger. Without thought, she walked over to the woman and physically slapped the food from her hand.

Addiction was starting to change Linda. Her life was driven more and more by the need for drugs and therefore the need for money. Everything always seemed to be moving at warp speed around her, and Linda fought hard to keep up.

The pattern that Linda had fallen into over the years was redeveloping, and its consequence had become more severe. As Linda's drug use got worse, her family life suffered. Now that Emily was older, she was more aware of what was going on with her mother. While she hadn't yet figured out what her mom did for a living, she did understand that she was addicted to drugs. During this time, it became common-place for Emily to come home from school and find the entire living room rearranged. Furniture would be moved into odd locations and items from other areas of the house would sit where they previously had not. Sometimes she would find her mom on her hands and knees on the floor, violently scrubbing at the wood or tile. For Emily and her sister, this was a sign their mother had been taking drugs again. By the time Emily was nearing the end of middle school, she knew to expect this behavior from time to time and had grown proficient at ignoring it.

CHAPTER 26

By EARLY 1995, THE City of Saint Paul had begun investigating the Cosmos Sauna again. Having successfully shut down the Como Rice Health Club and managing to run a number of other sex-for-money businesses out of the city, officials were ready to continue their triumphs.

Undercover operations started again with a five-person arrest on January 5, 1995, at Cosmos. Throughout the year, smaller operations netted prostitution arrests and convictions all around the city.

In the fall of 1995, police began conducting surveillance outside the Cosmos Sauna. On December 27, 1995, a police sergeant stopped a man leaving the business. The customer reported that upon entry, he had paid $100 to be let past security. After taking a shower, he was met by a woman named Bridgett*. She told him that he needed to make her feel comfortable, and the man subsequently performed oral sex on Bridgett. He paid her an additional $40, and Bridgett gave him a blow job and had sex with him.

A few weeks later, on January 9, 1996, two police officers again surveilled the Cosmos. They stopped a customer leaving who reported that he performed oral sex on a woman inside the building on his first visit but that this time he paid a woman named Bridgett $100 for oral sex. He wasn't asked to perform oral sex on the woman because he had done it previously.

A week later, the operation stepped up and an officer went in undercover. Inside the Cosmos sauna, the officer was greeted and taken into a room by a woman named Holly*. As Holly reclined next to him on the bed, she told the officer that he needed to make her feel comfortable and made a gesture indicating oral sex. Holly went on to say that all new customers had to do this. The officer told Holly he thought this was disgusting and he did not want to do it. But, as she was leaving the room, Holly turned back and asked what the officer was looking for, and he told her a "half and half." Holly told him that would cost him $140, and he handed her the cash. She left the room and returned with a condom.

Holly then removed her dress and G-string panties and began giving the officer a massage on his buttocks. She rolled him over and put the condom in her mouth while she began to rub his penis. As Holly leaned down to put the condom on his penis with her mouth, she was informed that she was under arrest.

On February 22, 1996, officers stopped customers leaving the Cosmos again. Both men admitted to paying for oral sex or intercourse and reported that they were asked to perform oral sex to prove they were not police officers.

Now, the police had enough information to request a warrant. On February 25, 1996, warrants were signed to search the Cosmos Sauna and Linda Spencer's home.

■ ■ ■

LINDA HADN'T BEEN UNAWARE of what was going on. She had seen the police watching her home again and knew of the arrests that happened at her business, but she'd nearly grown used to that. She was careful to pay attention to her surroundings and always kept a strict watch on the women working in her sauna. More than ever, Linda couldn't afford to lose her business—it had become her sole source of income.

One evening, Linda received a call at home. The man on the other end of the phone was crystal clear: "Burn it all." She'd received warning calls before. More than once she had packed up her daughters and gone to spend the night in a hotel for fear of being arrested, but this call was different. Never had she been told to destroy anything. Linda lit a fire immediately and got to work.

Into the flames went client cards she'd brought home and the receipts collected from the safes over the course of the last twenty years. She tossed in bank statements and handwritten notes, job applications, and employee paperwork. For hours she collected paper stored in her house and watched it burn. Linda was nervous, but in the back of her mind, she never thought they would come for her. It had been too long; she'd done too much. If they hadn't come by now, they probably never would. And even if they did, she had succeeded in avoiding prosecution in the past, and she would be able to do it again.

But on March 1, 1996, Linda's luck ran out. She was leaving the Cosmos Sauna after a long day. She was driving her four-door sedan, and David was following behind her in her van. Just a few blocks down Rice Street after pulling out of Cosmos, David and Linda were pulled over. Officers arrested Linda on the spot for suspicion of promoting prostitution.

After taking Linda into custody, the Saint Paul Police were able to execute their warrant and take over the Cosmos Sauna, much like they had done previously at the Como Rice Health Club. Female officers entered the sauna to pose as employees and began what they called a "decoy operation." During the time they were operating the business, undercover officers arrested three men for engaging in prostitution after they attempted to pay the officers for sex.

A few days later, police came back to execute a search warrant. During the search, officers went into the upper level at 843, the space where Tom had lived, which was now set up as an office. Officers found a desk, bookcase, chair, and lamp along with bills addressed to the Cosmos and guest receipts identical to the ones used downstairs. They were particularly interested in the monitors and cables set up on the desk upstairs. The officers noticed that the cables ran directly through the floor and into the lower level of the building. With one officer downstairs and one up, they pulled and tugged on the cables until they were able to confirm that they led to and from the cameras installed in the hallway of the sauna. There were no cameras in the individual rooms, only the hallways, so there would be no charge for recording the sexual activities that were bought and sold in the rooms behind the doors.

Using all of the information they had gathered, along with the recent convictions, the Ramsey County Attorney's Office prepared a notice to abate nuisance. Conviction notices had been sent as required by the law to Tom and Linda as the building owners and business operators, and now they were both served with a public nuisance complaint. With the criminal case against Linda running tandem to a civil suit, the City of Saint Paul had a great chance of succeeding in closing the Cosmos Sauna this time.

■ ■ ■

ON APRIL 29, 1996, a 22-page criminal complaint was filed in Ramsey County District Court against Linda May Spencer, Thomas Beier, and David. Each of the three defendants were charged with four criminal counts: one count each for promotion of and aiding and abetting in the promotion of prostitution and three counts each for racketeering. Police had been able to provide prosecutors with enough evidence to prove that Linda, Tom, and David had each participated in the promotion of prostitution through hiring employees to work in the Cosmos and knowingly providing a place for, and receiving proceeds from, acts of prostitution. Moreover, the business was being operated for the purpose of prostitution, giving rise to the racketeering charges.

Just days after the criminal complaint was filed, the Twin Cities media picked up on the case. No longer could Linda lead a double life. Now, everyone knew who she was and what she did. She had been charged with the same crimes Rand had famously gone to jail for years earlier, and people in the community began to take note. Her now teenage girls were suddenly brutally aware of the truth Linda had hidden from them for so long. In one fell swoop, her daughters learned that both of their parents were undeniably pimps.

CHAPTER 27

As the stakes became higher, Linda became bolder. Rather than giving up, closing her business, and quietly making a deal with prosecutors, Linda made the decision to fight again. She hired S. Mark Vaught to defend her in criminal court and continued to run her business as if it would last forever.

While Tom began trying to separate himself from the business both in court and by spending less time at the property, Linda continued to run it and stopped shying away from what it was she was doing there. While her daughters lost friends, while neighbors turned the other way, Linda stood tall and strong, insistent on fighting as long as it took. She'd successfully held the city off for almost twenty years. As those around her gave up and gave in, she'd remained there, continuing to fight off their persistent advances. Three storefront saunas remained in Saint Paul. Alongside Linda stood Lee Lenore and the owner of the Emporium Sauna. They would fight until the bitter end, and Linda planned to fight with them.

But the City of Saint Paul would not rest on its laurels this time. With Linda facing criminal charges and her building facing closure for nuisance, the police continued monitoring the building and obtaining convictions. As if needing to nail closed the coffin in which Linda lay, the Saint Paul Police continued undercover busts and outside stops in March, April, May, June, and July of 1996. And although by the end of September, a temporary injunction had been issued precluding prostitution at 843 Rice Street, the police made one final arrest on October 11, 1996, after a man paid $100 for a hand job.

Finally, the week before Christmas in 1996, Linda made the difficult decision to close down her business for good. Vaught had advised Linda that her plea negotiations and eventual sentencing would have a better outcome if she were able to tell prosecutors and the judge that she had closed the business. If the City of Saint Paul felt it had won, it would be less inclined to push for a trial or long sentence.

Twenty years of a hard-fought battle came to an end.

The City had finally won. Linda had been a business owner, an entrepreneur in her own right, and while her craft was not one of high moral standing, it had supported her. It supported her family and gave them a life she'd dreamed of providing them. Without the sauna, Linda didn't know what she would do for work or how she would make her house payment and put food on the table for her daughters.

■ ■ ■

THE DAY BEFORE CHRISTMAS Eve in 1996 was the day Linda May Spencer would plead guilty for her crimes. Her lawyer had spent time negotiating the plea deal with the prosecutor, and Linda had at long last relented. She couldn't fight anymore. The cost alone had become too much to handle. In court that day, attorney Mark Vaught laid out the agreement for the judge:

> I will state it. Then Mr. McLaughlin can sup-
> plement if he feels necessary. And that is … the
> defendant will plead guilty to count I of the com-
> plaint, that being the violation of committing the
> offense of promotion of prostitution in violation
> of Minnesota Statutes 609.322, subdivision 32
> and 609.321, subdivision 7, as well as 609.05. In
> addition, she would plead guilty to count II of
> the complaint. That is an offense constituting the

offense of racketeering in violation of Minnesota statutes 609.903, subdivision 11, and again 609.05. The State will dismiss counts III and IV of the complaint.

And we have also discussed the issue of sentencing. The State is to remain mute on the issue of jail sentence.

I have discussed with Ms. Spencer the various discussions had by the parties and the attorneys for the parties and the Court here also that the State will seek no fine, no real estate forfeiture; that she has agreed that as a condition that the business is to remain permanently closed and will represent today that the business has already been closed. She is, as a condition of the plea, to dispose of any remaining interest she might have in the business itself, which I suspect is moot because the business is already closed; that any probation time, the agreement with the State, would be capped at 10 years.

And with respect to the actual sentencing, my discussions with the Court would leave me to believe the Court intends to treat it with respect to the sentencing guidelines, with the exception of probation, as they would treat the underlying promotion of prostitution. The other conditions of probation are to be decided by the Court after a presentence investigation.[2]

Linda was then asked to step to the front of the courtroom, where the Honorable Lawrence D. Cohen asked for her plea.

How do you plead, Linda May Spencer, to count I of the complaint charging you with the charge of promotion of prostitution in Ramsey County, Minnesota, between the dates of January 1990 and March of 1996? Do you plead guilty or not guilty?

"Guilty," Linda said.

How do you plead to count II of that complaint, namely, racketeering, between January of 1990 and March of 1996 in Ramsey County, Minnesota, guilty or not guilty?

Again, Linda said, "Guilty." She was then seated in the witness box and sworn in to testify regarding the complaint

---

2 Transcript of Plea Proceedings, December 23, 1996, Ramsey County Courthouse, Saint Paul, MN. Originally transcribed by Roger J. Carter, Jr., Certified Court Reporter.

and her pleas. Through his questions, Vaught established that Linda understood the charges against her and that she was voluntarily making a guilty plea to each. He also made sure Linda understood that through her plea she was giving up her right to a trial by jury and the chance to bring any witnesses to testify on her behalf.

After Mr. Vaught walked Linda through the entire plea process, Judge Cohen spoke directly to her:

Ms. Spencer, I have informed the attorneys here that I was going to go along with all of the conditions that are set forth on the petition here, but there are three things that you are going to have to do for me. Number one, you are going to have to show up at the time and the place of sentencing. Do you understand that?

"Yes, I do," Linda said.

Number two, you must fully and completely cooperate with the probation department in the presentence investigation. Do you understand that?

"Yes." She nodded.

And lastly, no more messing around. No more of

the activity or conduct that led you to be sitting where you now are. Do you understand that?

"I understand that," Linda said to the judge.

"Now, you do those three things, I go along completely with this," he said sternly.

"Okay."

If you violate any one of those three things, you then get a different story. Then your plea of guilty will continue to stand, and I would not be bound by the plea agreement, and I could sentence you in accordance with the state law. Do you understand that?

"Yes, I do," Linda said.

The judge accepted and entered Linda's guilty pleas, but the hearing wasn't over. She now had to testify to the facts to which she was pleading guilty. Assistant Ramsey County Attorney Stephen McLaughlin questioned Linda:

"Ms. Spencer, good morning."

"Good morning," Linda replied.

"Can you tell me how long you have been involved with a business called the Cosmos, which is located at 843 Rice Street in Ramsey County, Minnesota?"

"Cosmos?" Linda asked.

"Yes."

"Quite a long time."

"Has it been since at least January of 1990?"

"Yes."

"Okay. And do you own that real property?"

"Yes."

"And are you aware that at least three incidents of prostitution have occurred at that property which you own since January of 1990?"

"Yes."

"And can you tell the Court what your role was with regard to the business? Can you describe that to the Court?"

"I ran the business."

"Okay. Did you hire and fire certain female employees who were managers?"

"Yes."

"Did you pick up the cash proceeds of the business?"

"Yes."

"You paid taxes with regard to the business?"

"Yes."

"Did you bail out certain employees who were arrested for prostitution charges?"

"Yes."

"And you managed the business at first when you were married with Mr. Beier; is that correct?"

"He managed it, yes."

"And later you managed the business, after that marriage dissolved, with [David]; is that correct?"

"Not really. I mostly ran it."

Vaught had three questions for Linda. He wanted the judge to know that Linda was no longer conducting business of any kind.

"The business at 843 Rice Street has been closed, has it not?"

"Yes."

"When was that closure?"

"I believe a week."

"And it's your intent that that be permanently closed, is that correct?"

"Definitely," Linda said.

There would be about three months before Linda's sentencing. While she knew the prosecutor did not intend to ask for jail time, there was no guarantee the judge would go along with the proposed probationary sentence. He had made himself clear that Linda had better stay out of trouble.

▪ ▪ ▪

FOR THEIR PARTS, BOTH Tom and David had been able to plead to lesser crimes than Linda. Perhaps as a thank you for their cooperation or maybe because they truly had been accessories to Linda's wrongdoings, both men were ultimately convicted of gross misdemeanor crimes.

Tom and David pled guilty to receiving profits from prostitution and both served short probations.

Between her plea hearing and sentencing was some of the most difficult time in Linda's life. She had no source of income, drugs were not easy to come by because the money she did have she needed for food, and the feelings and emotions of the last twenty years were suddenly washing over her. She had no way to prevent the onslaught of feelings; now she was forced to reflect on all she'd experienced and all she had lost.

Linda often found herself thinking of the women she had employed. She'd tried hard to remain disconnected from them. She didn't want to feel for them, but she did. Even though she didn't ask, she knew their stories. Many of them came from childhoods like her own; many of them were working for her only to provide for their own children and families. Now, she feared these women would turn to the streets to find work. They would put themselves in danger to make a fraction of the money they had while working for her. Pimps would find and exploit these women, and some of them would lose their lives.

Linda understood that what she did was not that different from a pimp on the surface. She paid women to have sex with men. That was simple. But unlike a pimp, Linda never broke her women. She did not hurt them, she did not manipulate them, she did not ever keep them against their will. The women who came to Linda for work wanted to work for her. Linda gave them safety, she gave them steady work, and in the end, she gave them care. Whether she was strict or lenient, Linda was their boss, and she provided those women with employment and protection. Now, there was nothing she could do to help them.

Weighing on her most during that time was her family. Linda felt horrible for the things she had done to her daughters. While she had been so determined to protect them, she had put them in the middle of the mess she had created. In losing her husband, Linda had sent her girls to the unkind arms of another woman, one who didn't want them. In losing her business, she'd left her daughters with nothing—no legacy, no pride, and most importantly, no mother to take care of them. If she went to jail, Linda didn't know what would happen to her daughters.

CHAPTER 28

MARCH 17, 1997, TWO decades after she became a madam, Linda May Spencer walked into the Ramsey County Courthouse to be sentenced for her crimes. The City of Saint Paul had won. Linda no longer owned property in the city; her final certificate of occupancy for the building at 843 Rice had been revoked in January. The fight was over.

Linda stood nervously at the front of the courtroom alongside her attorney. She was terrified that she would be sentenced to jail. Despite the agreement she'd made with the prosecutor that she would only be sentenced to probation, she knew the judge had the power to make his own decision.

During the time between the two hearings, Linda was required to participate in a presentence investigation. Even the investigator was aware that Linda's career was over and she was going to need to essentially start over. Linda discussed with the investigator the possibility of going to veterinary school. She'd always loved animals and Linda thought this would be a career path that would interest and fulfill her. The judge took a particular interest in this when reviewing the presentence investigator's notes. He told Linda it would be a hard path but that he respected her decision to take it.

Finally, the sentencing began. The crime of promotion of prostitution carried a minimum sentence of one year and one day in the State of Minnesota. This meant Linda would be sentenced to a minimum of 366 days in prison. This was a felony offense. Linda had also pled guilty to and was in court to be sentenced for racketeering, a second felony offense for which 366 days of prison were a minimum. She was acutely aware of the possibility that she would be handcuffed and led to jail right from the courtroom that day. Linda held her breath as the judge began.

In plea negotiations, the State of Minnesota, through the Ramsey County Attorney's Office, had agreed not to recommend any jail time; the State would ask for only probation for Linda. Luckily, the judge at her sentencing hearing agreed. While there were many conditions of her probation that the court would now discuss, Linda knew then that she would be permitted to walk out of the courtroom that day and go home. Relief washed over her as she listened to the judge speak.

As a special condition of probation, you are to abstain from the use of all drugs, all chemicals, or anything of a mood-altering nature. You are to attend AA meetings weekly. You are subject to random UAs. And the Court is going to order you to do 100 hours of community service. You are entitled to six days custody credit.

Linda was not assessed any fees or fines.

Continuing to list probation conditions that were specific to Linda's case, Judge Cohen said:

Okay. In addition to that, Ms. Spencer, you are to have no involvement with any escort service, sauna service, or massage service. You are to have no participation directly or indirectly in any manner with anything even remotely close to prostitution or any of these other items that I have said. You are to have no contact with any former parlor employees, except you may have contact with [Tom]. You are not to have any contact with any known prostitute …

When it was all said and done, Linda was sentenced to ten years of probation for the two felony charges. She would serve no time in prison. She had gotten off quite lucky.

As the hearing drew to a close, Judge Cohen addressed Linda directly:

"Do me a favor, Ms. Spencer. Don't come back to court. Deal?"

"A deal," she replied.[3]

---

3 Transcript of Sentencing Proceedings, March 17, 1997, Ramsey County Courthouse, Saint Paul, MN. Originally transcribed by Roger J. Carter, Jr., Certified Court Reporter.

PART 3

CHAPTER 29

THE END DIDN'T COME on March 17, 1997 for Linda. In many ways, it was just the beginning of her plummet. She hadn't hit bottom. The next ten years would be a steady descent into the depths of a place she had never even come close to before.

As she stood there that day, discussing her plans to attend veterinary school and promising the judge she wouldn't return to court, Linda was high. She'd turned to cocaine that day to calm her nerves and to ease what she believed would be the inevitable pain of her first night in prison.

The truth was Linda knew she'd probably never make it to vet school. She could dream of it, even talk about it, but in reality, if nothing else, she'd never be able to afford it. After all she'd been through, despite the money she had made in her businesses, Linda was broke. She'd paid legal fees for civil defense, criminal defense, and for her divorce. She'd mortgaged her building and put everything she had up for collateral. Now, she'd given up her business, and she had nothing left.

One thing that Linda did know was that she needed to find a job. She'd need a source of income to put food on the table. But finding a job with felony convictions on your record is not easy. When she completed her community service hours, Linda started to look for work.

Although she had been a successful business owner, Linda had few skills that would translate to real-world work experience. She'd never taken the time to upgrade technologies in her saunas, so she was not versed in keyboarding, computers, or even cash registers. She was unprepared to work in an office and would need training to work in any store.

Eventually, Linda came to the realization that her once-lavish lifestyle was over. She would have to take a job in a factory if she was going to be able to feed her children and keep her house. Soon Linda found work at an airplane parts manufacturing factory not far from home as a press operator. It wasn't easy work and Linda despised having to punch a timeclock, but after a while, she settled into the reality of her new life.

Ten years of probation would mean ten years of keeping her nose clean, so Linda tried hard to get sober. She'd been used to the life of fast cash and easy drugs, but now she would have struggled to find money to support her habit anyway. For a while, Linda put her head down and worked hard to earn her living like everyone else in her world.

■ ■ ■

IT WASN'T LONG AFTER losing her business and being convicted that the IRS came looking for Linda May Spencer. She'd fought long and hard in her divorce for what she believed was rightfully hers, but when the taxes went unpaid, the IRS came looking for the owner; and because Linda had fought so hard for the business, it was her. With hundreds of thousands of dollars in tax liens, Linda knew she'd never again get ahead.

As much as she tried to leave the past behind her, Linda could not. The financial fallout from her business was beginning to creep back, and she was forced to revisit the complicated feelings she'd been trying to bury. So Linda turned to the only thing she knew would dull her pain. With less money to spend, cocaine was not going to be an option for her. Instead, Linda went in search of heroin.

Cocaine and heroin both numbed Linda's pain but in significantly different ways. A line of coke made Linda fly.

She went fast on cocaine. But heroin is a depressant with a much different effect than the cocaine high she truly craved. When Linda injected heroin, it slowed her down. What used to be an unstoppable force became a sluggish and sad woman.

Heroin was cheaper to buy, but it required more accoutrements than cocaine. What she could previously snort up her nose now needed to be injected with a needle. One evening in November of 1997, Linda had heroin but no way to inject it. She desperately needed the high, and so she made her way to a drugstore in search of needles.

Once inside the pharmacy, Linda broke into the locked display that held syringes for medical use and put a package in her purse. What she didn't realize was that a store employee had seen her do this and called the police. As Linda exited the store, she was approached by officers. When they asked if she had taken anything from the store, Linda admitted that she had and allowed the officers to search her purse. Inside they found the stolen syringes along with the heroin she was planning to inject. Linda was arrested and taken to jail.

This incident could have had catastrophic consequences for Linda. One of the conditions of her probation was that she remain law abiding. Any criminal activity and convictions during the ten years of her probationary term could result in the revocation of the probation. A revoked probation for Linda would send her straight to prison.

After all she had lost, Linda could no longer afford to arm herself with a criminal defense attorney like S. Mark Vaught. Now she would ask for the services of a court-appointed public defender, leaving her slightly less confident that she would come out unscathed.

By April of 1998, the public defender appointed to serve as Linda's attorney was able to work out a plea deal for her that would satisfy the court and allow her to stay out of prison a little longer. Linda pled guilty to one of the four charges that had been entered against her and agreed to pay restitution to the pharmacy for the damage she'd caused. She also agreed to participate in a community service program in lieu of spending time in jail. Now, she would be serving probation in two separate counties in the state but once again was lucky to avoid jail or prison. Linda had gotten off easy, but it was more important than ever that she stay out of trouble and out of court.

CHAPTER 30

THE THING ABOUT ADDICTION is that it doesn't care why you are trying to fight it. Addiction doesn't take ten years off to let you raise your kids or allow you to serve out your probation. Addiction is a disease and without proper treatment, it will take from its host until there is nothing left to give.

Linda spent the years of her probation trying to get by. She fought and gave in to the power of her addiction time and time again, using when she had money to use and trying to get clean when the spirit moved her. It was a constant and lonely battle for which Linda's friends and family had little tolerance.

Throughout the years, while she ran her business successfully, Linda's family never turned their backs on her. At different times she employed her siblings in various ways; her mother had even been helpful with accounting during the time when Linda was managing the properties alone. It wasn't that she counted on them for help, but she felt a part of them, and never felt they looked down on her for her choices. But when it all ended, Linda suddenly found herself the focus of contempt from her siblings. Her brother, who had an unsuccessful run as a security worker at the Cosmos due to his inability to separate business from pleasure, now judged Linda for her choices. Her sister, who had enjoyed many of the perks of Linda's financial successes, including taking advantage of her access to drugs, now acted as if Linda was weak for her inability to quit. When she needed them the most, Linda's family abandoned her.

There was only one member of her family who was willing to stay by her side and help her during this time. For all she had failed to provide her in the past, Margaret stepped up when Linda was in dire straits. Not unlike she and Tom, Linda and her mother seemed to trade sobriety over the years. When Linda was deep in her drug use, it was often her mother who would come and try to bring her back. Likewise, when Margaret fell into alcoholism, Linda took care of her.

There wasn't much Margaret could offer her daughter during this time, but there was one thing she was willing to do to protect her. As the IRS bore down on Linda, trying to collect back taxes for years of income, Linda and her mother made a plan. Margaret would buy Linda's home from her and allow her to live there and let Linda pay the mortgage through her. This would give Linda the ability to stay in her home with her daughters at least until they graduated from high school and moved on to their own lives.

They weren't as clever as they thought, though. Linda and her mother were eventually asked to go to court and explain what it was they were attempting to do and prove that it was not an effort to avoid the tax liens pending against Linda. She and Margaret went to court without an attorney and basically played dumb. Linda put on an Academy Award–winning performance in court, saying things to the judge like "How could you accuse this elderly woman who served thirty years as a police officer of trying to scam the government?" Somehow, it worked, and the judge approved the sale. Now Linda was living in her own home, but with her mother as her landlord.

■ ■ ■

MARGARET HAD ENDURED A lifetime of depression when she finally decided to seek treatment. Medication helped regulate her feelings and also led her to sobriety. In Linda's opinion, it allowed her to become close with her mother during a time when her own life was largely out of control. When Margaret was diagnosed with lung cancer in 2006, it was a devastating blow to Linda. She never thought her relationship with her mother would be fully repaired, but they had come to a place where they better understood each other, and she finally felt love from her mom.

She'd been dabbling in drugs again when she learned her mother was sick, but this news sent Linda into a tailspin. She immediately fell deep into addiction, attempting to get high as frequently as possible and by any means necessary.

On October 17, 2006, while her mother suffered the effects of cancer, Linda was stopped while driving in a suburb of Saint Paul. In her vehicle, officers uncovered a large amount of marijuana, enough to believe she may be transporting it for sale. Once again, Linda was arrested. Unlike in the past, now there was no one jumping to help bail Linda out. She spent three nights in the Dakota County Jail before she had a hearing and was released to return for further court dates.

Linda was just months away from the end of her probation when this arrest occurred. She was again faced with the possibility of her probation being revoked and potentially being sent to jail. She was terrified. She took a deal offered by the prosecutor to plead guilty to possession in exchange for a new probation and significant amount of public service. A sentencing hearing was scheduled for February 12, 2007. Linda knew from her experience that the judge may not agree with the plea deal she had worked out and there was still a chance she could be sentenced to jail.

But as Linda's mother got sicker and her sentencing date drew closer, she found herself again spinning out of control. She was using drugs and alcohol, doing anything she could think of to numb the pain of what was to come. She feared nothing more than the possibility that she might be in a jail cell while her mother took her last breath.

It was one week before she was due in court for her sentencing when it all became too much to bear. Linda drank and got so high she hardly knew what she was doing as she got in her car to go to her dealer's house to buy more drugs. When she arrived, no one answered the door, so, in her state of desperation, Linda kicked in the window. After realizing there would be no way she could get inside, even with the broken window, a bloodied Linda got in her car and went home.

Hours later, there was a knock on her door. The police were standing on her porch. Linda opened the door and spoke with the officers, obviously intoxicated. Looking at her record, the officers saw that Linda was due in court in a week's time, and rather than taking her to jail, they wrote her citations for trespassing, criminal damage to property, and driving while intoxicated. As she closed the door and the officers left, Linda knew her fate was sealed.

CHAPTER 31

LINDA STOOD BEFORE THE judge in Dakota County on February 12, 2007, in tremendous emotional pain. Years and years of luck had run out, and she knew what she was facing. Her public defender could only do so much. Linda had agreed to plead guilty to the most recent drug charges, but now, with new crimes on her record, there wasn't much of a chance she could avoid jail.

The only hope she had, and the one thing that meant the most to her, was that the judge would take pity on Linda and allow her to report to jail after her mother had passed away. In the courtroom that day to help explain to the judge the situation was Linda's brother. When Linda's attorney asked if her brother could address the court to explain the circumstances, he turned on her.

He did explain that their mother was ill, that she had weeks, if not days, to live, but he went on. Linda's brother told the judge that he believed his sister should go to jail, that her problems had become bigger than her, and jail would be the only chance she might have to get control of her life again. Linda was angry. In her eyes, her brother had betrayed her at a time when she needed him most of all. After court that day, Linda would learn that it was her mother who had asked her brother to do that. It had been, in her mother's eyes, the only way to save Linda, but to her it had been a betrayal. Linda believed her brother and sisters were using her addiction as a way to take what was hers.

As Dakota County Judge David Knutson reviewed her history, he seemed to agree with her brother. He spoke to Linda directly from the bench, expressing his sympathy for her mother's illness but also his shock that up until that day, she had managed to avoid serving significant jail time. Judge Knutson told Linda that he agreed that a stay in jail might be a good time for her to find a way to make some changes in her life. He offered a reprieve in his final comments. As he sentenced Linda to ninety days in jail for felony possession of marijuana, he opted not to have her taken into custody from the courthouse that day. Instead, Judge Knutson said that Linda would report to jail on

February 26, 2007, by 6:00 p.m. or after her mother had passed, whichever came first.

As Linda left the courtroom, she was angry with her brother and with herself. She'd ruined her own life. She'd taken every chance she had and thrown it away, always thinking she'd get another one. This time, she had no more chances. All Linda had left in front of her were the death of her mother and a 90-day stay in jail.

While February 26 grew closer, Linda began to fear once again that she would be in a jail cell when her mother took her last breath. It became her greatest fear and something she couldn't bring herself to think about. She made a call to her public defender just days before she was due to report to jail to ask if there was any way she could get more time. Lucky for her, the lawyer was able to speak with the court and extend the report date by a few days.

Linda sat vigil at her mother's bedside in her final days. She'd spent so many years of her life driven by the need to be different than the woman who lay before her. For a woman who rarely showed love, it was remarkable for Linda to witness the outpouring of affection that had come for Margaret in the form of not only family but also friends.

Margaret fought hard in her final days and hours. She fought to remain alert and engage with visitors who came to say goodbye. As Linda sat with her mother, she witnessed many of the final conversations of her mother's life. She stood by and watched as her siblings said goodbye to their mother. She cried as she witnessed her own daughters kiss their grandmother one final time.

The experience brought Linda back to when her stepfather died. Charles Vaccaro and her mother had been married for about ten years; Linda was nineteen at the time. Charles has been a wonderful step-father, taking Margaret's children as his own and loving them the way a father should.

As she and her siblings waited with their mother at his deathbed, he'd said something to Margaret that Linda only partly understood then. Charles said, "Peg, you didn't do your job." Linda wondered in the moment what he meant. He went on, "You didn't do your job *as a mother*."

At the age of nineteen, Linda had agreed with Charles. Her mother hadn't done her job. She'd never given them comfort or love. She'd never given them guidance or structure. Her mother had been a figure in her life. She was a provider of food and shelter, but as a mother, she hadn't done her job.

Now, as she sat by her mother's deathbed, she wondered the same about herself. Had she done her job? She'd promised herself so many times that she wouldn't be like her own mother. She'd wanted to give her girls everything and for a long time, she had. But on that day, sitting there watching her mother fade away, Linda knew there were plenty of things she hadn't done right.

On February 27, 2007, Margaret Vaccaro passed away. She would be remembered as one of the first female police officers in Los Angeles County and an accomplished detective at the Minneapolis–St. Paul International Airport. She was the mother of six, grandmother to seven, and, upon her death, great-grandmother to five.

CHAPTER 32

LINDA HAD WORKED HARD to provide for her children. She made as much money as she could, she did her best to be home to have family dinner every night, and she hid all of her transgressions from her daughters. But it was in this battle that Linda lost herself. It was in her insistence to lead a double life that she found herself living somewhere in between them both, stuck with one foot on each side, desperately trying to stop herself from splitting in two.

Linda had never been the type of young girl who dreamed of growing up and being a mother. She didn't play with dolls or play house; she didn't have that maternal yearning that some of her friends did. The birth of her first daughter was actually Linda's fourth pregnancy. When she found out she was pregnant that time, it was different. She was in love with Tom and, suddenly, she did feel maternal. She wanted this baby and, before the baby was even born, she knew she wanted more.

But it was Linda's deep desire to bring her girls up in a home so different than the one she knew that became the main focus of her motherhood. Linda put pressure on herself to do so much that she often found herself barely able to do anything at all. She turned to cocaine to find the extra hours she needed in the day to do all she needed to accomplish.

When Linda reflects back, it is the guilt of motherhood that overwhelms her the most. She knows that when her girls were young, they understood that their mom was high. While six- and eight-year-old children may not be able to identify the reason for their mother's odd behavior, they can definitely recognize when it is happening. Linda remembers how many days she woke up from a night of drug use feeling sick and tired only to take that out on her daughters. She was impatient and quick to anger when her daughters needed her to be calm and comforting. She hurried them when they needed her to take time and lead them. Linda recognizes the reality of the life she gave them. And while she tries hard to let go of the guilt, it will never go away. As Emily looks into her eyes and tells her she forgives her and that Linda should no longer feel ashamed, she always will.

Linda experienced this pain from both sides. She is both the daughter of an addict and an addicted mother. She remembers the sadness she felt as a child when her mother would lock herself in her bedroom with a bottle. The fear and loneliness she felt compounds the guilt of knowing she did the same thing to her own daughters.

Sitting at her mother's deathbed was a humbling experience for Linda. Her own daughters were grown, like she to her mother. She'd given them as much as she could, but she knew it wasn't enough. She wrestled with the feelings she had for her mother while wondering if they were the same feelings her girls felt for her.

Margaret fought hard to find happiness in her life, to enjoy her elder years being a grandmother and great-grandmother. She made it known to her children that the depression she had suffered during their childhoods was something she was fighting off. She took medication and tried hard to battle the demons she carried. But there was Linda, holding the hand of a woman she had spent a lifetime blaming while she waited for her to die. When her mother took her last breath, Linda wouldn't be there to console her own daughters. She wouldn't mourn with her family and work to find a way through life without her mother. Instead, she would go to jail.

So, what kind of mother was she? As much as she had

tried to be different in so many ways, had she become exactly the same? Had she been worse? If it were her lying in the hospital bed nearing her last breath, would her daughters be there holding her hands?

■ ■ ■

A FEW DAYS AFTER HER mother's funeral, Linda turned herself in. She would serve her ninety days in the women's facility at the Ramsey County Adult Detention Center in Saint Paul. It was one of the hardest moments of her life. Having just lost her mother, Linda went into jail with a depression she'd never experienced before.

Unlike other nights Linda had spent in jail, this time she would be housed in the general population and would be assigned to a cell with another woman. She was unhappy to have lost the benefit of the isolation she previously enjoyed during her time as a madam. When Linda walked into her cell on her first night, carrying her blanket and pillow, she saw a woman sleeping on the bottom bunk. As is jail protocol, Linda tossed her stuff to the top and climbed up.

As she lay awake, trying to find sleep in the cold and unfamiliar surroundings, she heard a quiet humming. She sat straight up in her bed. The woman below her, the one who had been randomly assigned to be her cellmate for at least part of the next ninety days, was humming the song "You'll Never Find a Love Like Mine" by Lou Rawls. Her mother's favorite song. It was as if her mother had finally reached out and wrapped her arms around her to tell her everything was going to be okay. The tears came fast and endlessly. Linda lay back in her bed and let it all sink in. Her mother was gone, she was in jail, and nothing would ever be the same again.

Linda spent her days in jail introspectively. For the first time, she looked back on all the things she had done, rather than moving at warp speed away from them. Suddenly, Linda could see herself clearly as an addict, as a sex worker, and as a pimp. She could see the choices she had made and how one led to another, setting her off down a path of delinquency.

It was a brutal opportunity for Linda to look in the mirror and see the wrongs she had committed, not just in recent years but in her lifetime. Linda thought many days about the women who had worked for her and the men they had serviced. She thought about the drugs she had taken and the effects they had on her mind and body. She thought constantly about the family she had created and the marriage she'd lost. Time and time again, Linda found herself looking for someone to blame for the things she'd done and lost, but overwhelmingly she blamed herself.

Jail was a time in Linda's life when she would have benefited from a therapist of some kind. Her sobriety, albeit forced, allowed her to have a clear head, but without someone to direct her thinking, she only fell deeper into the depression that had always lived close to the surface.

Her self-loathing ate away at her inside the walls of the jail, leaving Linda as little more than a shell of herself as her release drew near.

One day while she was still inside, Linda heard her name during the mail call. Not knowing what to expect, she was surprised to see an envelope from an attorney's office. As it turned out, while she had been serving her time, her siblings were on the outside staging a coup. Because their mother had taken over the mortgage of Linda's home, her brother and sisters were able to make decisions about the house she planned to return to when she was free again. Without her authority, Linda's siblings had listed her house for sale and planned to split the proceeds among themselves. She had no means to fight them and even if she did, the IRS would have come for her. There was nothing Linda could do.

Aside from the torment she had inflicted on herself, her time in jail had been uneventful. After completing her sentence, Linda was released to a world she no longer recognized. She'd lost her mother, her daughters had moved on with their lives, and now, she would need to find a new place to live. Her siblings had been successful in selling her home.

CHAPTER 35

LINDA HAD BEEN OUT of jail for a couple of weeks, and still, she hadn't found work. She was going to lose her home in a few short days, and her family had turned on her. As hard as it was to find a job with a felony on her record, Linda had quickly learned that renting an apartment was even harder. She had no idea where she was going to go or what she was going to do.

She'd turned right back to drugs when she left jail. The three-month stay had sobered her, but it had also given her time to think. Linda never liked having time to think. This was one of the reasons she rarely drank. Linda hated being slowed down. So, she had found meth to be a better high for her than heroin—meth made her go fast, leaving her little time for thoughts of any kind.

She stayed at her old house, which had just sold, when she got out of jail, although, for the most part, it had fallen into disrepair. Before she was arrested, she spent nights there getting high, not taking care of the home that once protected her family. When she looked out the windows into the backyard, she no longer saw little girls playing; now she saw monkeys with guns hiding in the trees, products of the hallucinations and paranoia brought on by her drug use. Her life had spiraled far out of control.

On this day, Linda was packing. She had only a few days left before a new family would move into the home she once loved. When she came to a picture of her family from years earlier, she held it in her hand. Looking at it, she saw smiles. She saw two little girls, bright eyed and beaming at the camera. She saw herself—she was sober, happy, and loved. And finally, she saw Tom. He stood beside them all, smiling and protective, proud and excited to have those three beautiful people in his life. Now, they were all gone. No one smiled like that anymore, especially not Linda. She drew up her hand and smashed the picture to the ground. The glass from the frame shattered as it hit the wood beneath her feet.

She continued, moving room by room in an angry tirade. In one of the girls' rooms, Linda found a trophy won by a basketball team she had coached. She lifted it up from the desk where it sat and threw it against the wall. In the kitchen she pulled dishes from cabinets and smashed them to the floor. Old, faded artwork that clung to the refrigerator with magnets was ripped and crumbled.

She wanted drugs. She needed drugs to numb the pain she felt deep inside. She had none. She had no money to buy any. There was nothing left in the house, not a penny, not a crumb, not even a drip of old booze. There was nowhere for Linda to go and nothing she could do. She was stuck there inside the place that held everything she'd lost.

She called her daughters over and over. She alternated between them, begging one of them to answer. The endless ringing was answer enough. They'd seen too much, been through too much with their mother. She'd lost them too.

After they lost their grandmother, the girls had been contacted by Linda's siblings. They told her daughters they needed to get away from her—that she was ruining her own life and, by extension, theirs. In a time when she needed them the most, even her own daughters turned their backs on her, she thought.

Linda fell to the floor and cried into her hands, sobbing so uncontrollably that at times she could hardly breathe. She stood up and yelled. She threw her hands into the air and screamed. She called out to her mother, to her daughters, to her brother, Abby, to everyone and no one all at once.

No one came.

As she sat there on an uncovered mattress that lay on the floor among the mess she had made, she started to realize that perhaps she hadn't lost everything—maybe she had thrown it all away. She'd done this to herself. It was not her mother, not her father, not Tom or the police and judges—it was just her. She was the reason she was here. She had broken everything she touched.

Linda walked to the kitchen. Her mind was racing. She was completely and utterly alone. Her hands vacillated between her hair and her sides; her whole body trembled with fear and realization. She stood, leaning against the counter, rocking forward and back, until she saw a knife in the sink. It was balanced on a stack of dirty dishes that had been in the sink unwashed for days. Without thought, she darted across the kitchen and grabbed the knife.

As quickly as she picked it up, she brought it to her left wrist and cut. One straight line. It felt good. Moving up her forearm, she cut again. As the blood ran from her arm, relief washed over her. She wanted to feel more. She made a third cut, higher up her arm, and she watched the blood run down her hand and drip to the floor.

The feeling of the blood leaving her body was like being relieved of the burdens she carried. She watched as her failures spilled from her arm, a deep, dark crimson color.

She began to feel tired after a few minutes and made her way to the living room to lay on the couch. As she walked past the fireplace, she saw a towel soaking up rainwater that had leaked down the chimney. She took the towel and wrapped it around her arm. It was hot and humid in the house, but the water from the towel felt cool on her warm, bleeding skin.

Linda lay back, dangling her left arm off the side of the couch, and closed her eyes. She thought of her mom. Would she see her soon? Would they meet in heaven? Would either of them make it there? Had she or her own mother done any good in their lives that would lead them to a place of glory in the afterlife?

Would her girls be okay without her? They'd be better off—she knew that. As she felt the blood drip, she thought of the story her father told her about how she'd ruined his car, her blood was all over the trunk of his station wagon, but he'd saved her life anyway. She remembered those little brown spots in the carpet of his car. Was her blood making those same spots now? Would someone race to save her this time?

Linda could think of no reason to go on. As her body went numb and her thoughts drifted in and out of past and present, she surrendered. She let the fear and guilt, the pain and suffering, the good and the bad, all flow from her body with the blood that dripped from her arm.

She gave up and gave in to everything she'd spent so long trying to fight. She decided then that she wouldn't fight anymore. She was too tired to fight. So there, lying in her home, surrounded by shattered pieces of things she'd lost and all she'd thrown away, Linda May Spencer fell.

■ ■ ■

EMILY FLEW THROUGH THE front door of her childhood home. "Mom!" she yelled as she ran inside. "Mom!" she shrieked when she saw her. "Mom?"

She hadn't been ignoring her mother's calls. Emily had been at work. When she checked her cell phone at the end of her shift, she had twenty-eight missed calls from her mom. Listening to the voicemails, she was horrified. Message after message Linda screamed and cried. Each time she played another, Emily heard her mother say she was going to kill herself, that she had nothing left to live for. Emily immediately got into her car and drove toward the house she grew up in. As she drove, she called her sister and her boyfriend.

Emily was the first to arrive. As much as she didn't want to go inside alone, she couldn't stand to wait outside until her sister arrived. She was sure her mother had tried to kill herself, and she didn't know if she was already too late. As she bent over her barely breathing mother, she was filled with emotion. Emily was terrified, devastated, and furious all at once.

When her sister arrived, they made the decision to get Linda into the car and take her to the hospital. Even if they could stop the bleeding on their own, she needed more than that. Emily's mother needed more help than she could give her.

Once she was admitted and the bleeding subsided, Linda was placed on a 72-hour psychological hold, she would not be permitted to leave the hopsital even if she watned to. The doctors determined that she was a danger to herself. Linda could not be trusted to leave the hospital and be alone. She needed to be stabilized, both physically and emotionally.

Linda tried, more than once, to leave the hospital. She wanted to go home, she wanted to get back to drugs, she didn't want to be there dealing with the reality of what she had done. It took a few days before Linda came to terms with her situation. She admitted, finally, that she had intended to kill herself that night. She talked with a therapist at the hospital who understood the gravity of her depression and wanted to help her. Linda was put on medication to manage her mental health, and she felt hopeful for the first time in a long time.

■ ■ ■

LINDA HAD DRAWN A line in the sand. She'd chosen life. But to get to the other side of the line, she would first have to go back and examine the things that brought her to it and find a way to make it across.

Drugs had been a part of Linda's life since she was a child. From her first line of cocaine when she was fourteen years old until her last hit of meth, she'd lived so much of her life high. Drugs drove her. It had been her need for drugs that led to her career, her marriage, her success, and ultimately her downfall. But a life of sobriety scared Linda.

How, without drugs, would she mask the guilt and the pain she felt so deeply?

Looking back, she could see the things she'd used drugs to get through. In school, drugs made her feel included; they gave her common ground with the people around her. As she grew, drugs became part of her life; she was constantly surrounded by them. Drugs masked the fear of living on the edge.

When Linda ran her businesses, drugs blinded her. They let her see only what her mind could handle. When things came into focus, Linda could turn to her drugs to blur them again.

She even turned to drugs in her parenting. Rather than fight the guilt of feeling sick and tired in the morning, she would use drugs to calm and numb her. Instead of being too tired after a long day at work, she used drugs to get her through dinner and homework and bedtime. Drugs helped her transition from mother to madam and gave her the ability to be both for so many years.

To find her way to the other side of the line she had drawn, to live life clearly, Linda needed to leave drugs behind. She would need to find something else to comfort her and ease her pain. She would need to find something else to motivate her to work hard and make money. There would need to be something in Linda's life that she craved as much as drugs. This was when Linda found her higher power.

She has never defined her "higher power" or given it a name. On rare occasion, she will use the word "he," but most often, she simply says, "higher power." Linda fiercely believes in her higher power. It is one that guides her every move and protects her at all times.

She credits her higher power with her successes and leaves her failures to the higher power's plan for her. There is nothing she can't fit into this all-encompassing box.

In 2007 when Linda made the choice to live, she stopped her fall. In order to get all the way up, she needed to quit using drugs. Getting sober isn't easy for anyone, and Linda was no exception. There were slips along the way, relapses when it seemed she was headed back down. But once Linda set her sights on life, she refused to give in. She fought through the hard times and pressed through the slips, never letting them add up to a fall.

Giving herself to a higher power was part of this process for Linda. She needed something or someone to lean on when she felt weak. She needed a place to put her failures and something to believe in more than herself. Her higher power made her feel safe and loved unconditionally. With it, she could go on.

❚ ❚ ❚

ONE DAY, LINDA WOKE up in her car. The driver's side door was open, and she was slumped over the steering wheel. Slowly lifting her aching head, Linda realized her car was off of the road and in a grassy ditch. She was somewhere near Minneapolis, or at least that's what she thought.

Searching her mind, she couldn't find a strong memory of the night before, but she knew she had driven to Minneapolis to score some heroin. She'd needed it bad. The last thing she remembered was the needle in her arm.

She quickly took stock. Looking down, yes—she was wearing all of her clothes. Looking right, yes—her purse was on the passenger's seat, wallet sticking up from the unzipped top. Pulling down the visor, no—it did not appear that she had been beaten up. Keys? Yes—still in the ignition.

She rested her head back. How did she get here? How was it possible she had not been robbed, raped, or, worse, arrested? She had no idea. Closing her eyes, she took a deep breath. "Higher power," she said as she exhaled.

CHAPTER 36

THIS COULD HAVE BEEN the end for Linda. She could have been murdered; she could have overdosed or taken heroin laced with something that killed her. She'd been lucky, again. Lucky enough to be able to start her car and drive away. She knew she was being watched over. There was never any doubt in her mind—but she also knew at some point soon, her luck would run out.

On and off over the next few years, Linda lived with her daughters. She struggled to make ends meet because the only jobs she could get were low paying. Housing was nearly impossible to find due to her criminal record.

It was a meager existence, and Linda often felt the pressure and guilt of depending on her daughters for so much. But she continued to work on herself and her sobriety. She continued to fight through slips and push herself to regain her balance.

And she did slip. Waking in her car having survived a night on drugs she couldn't remember wasn't her last visit with substance abuse. There were other times, too. On more than one occasion, Emily came home to find her mother missing, only to locate her later—high on meth.

It took a long time for Linda to finally reach sobriety. She'd spent so long justifying her actions and giving herself excuses—she needed to learn to be easier on herself and harder at the same time. She had to learn to forgive the people in her past and also herself in order to find a way forward.

Taking a big fall isn't always the end, and getting back up isn't always the beginning. Sometimes it takes more than one fall. Sometimes it takes people helping you up. For Linda, it was only herself. Her fall and her slips and slides were her own doing. She accepts that. She owns her choices and her failures, and she has learned to forgive herself for most of them.

Linda knows she still doesn't stand on steady ground. An addict is always recovering but never recovered. She has to take each day as it comes and find her own balance when the ground shakes. Her stability is in her own hands.

■ ■ ■

WHEN LINDA SITS AND reflects, she can bring herself right back. She can smell the talcum powder, hear the whipping, taste the cocaine. It's never far from her mind. Those days were not few and far between. They were not lost. They were days earned and days lived, and they were days of hard work and hard love. She can reminisce in joy and in pain for that time in her life.

Linda May Spencer fought for twenty years against an entire institution set on running her out. Sometimes she had allies, and other times she fought alone. In all that time, she never backed down, never took a step back, and never caved to threats. She stood strong, taking fire from all sides over and over again.

And while she certainly has regrets and what-ifs, she also has good memories and pride. Linda is proud of the fight—proud of herself for never giving up or giving in. She knows that things could have been different had she made other decisions. But she knows she was successful in her own right. Linda is proud to call herself a Fallen Woman because she knows in the end, she got back up.

AFTERWORD

By: Emily Jean

I THINK TO MOST PEOPLE family represents stability, foundation, and comfort. An escape from the harshness of life—family is that place most can go for a sense of security. Not for me. My family represents chaos, stress, instability, and drama.

I don't like to reflect on my childhood. That's not to say it was all bad. I do have fond memories. But it is with the benefit of hindsight that I am often struck by the realization that some of the things I enjoyed the most were directly related to the business my parents owned.

The four of us used to spend nights at the Embassy Suites hotel in downtown Saint Paul. My sister and I would spend hours running through the open hallways and foyers playing hide and go seek. Back then, we didn't realize that Mom and Dad took us there because someone had tipped them off about police coming to search our house. To us, to me, it was a vacation from the ordinary life we lived at home.

One time, though, I remember coming home to a house that looked like a tornado had come through it. All of the furniture had been pushed around, drawers and cabinets emptied and left open with their contents thrown all around. When I close my eyes, I can still see the exact pattern of the muddy boot prints that covered the floor. Everything was a mess. I remember running to my bedroom hoping with everything I had that my room had been saved from this disaster. Flooded with relief, I cried when I saw that both my room and my sister's room had been untouched by whatever had happened in our house.

Looking back now things make more sense. I remember my friends weren't allowed to come to my home anymore. In some cases I wasn't allowed to play with my friends in the neighborhood or from my school. I remember things changed. Fewer people coming around, the strange looks from my teachers and kids at school that made me feel anxious and scared. It was difficult for me to focus in school.

I knew something was wrong; I just never understood what it was. Now I know that these were the times when my mother was in the news. When the neighbors read stories about her being a madam and saw police cars lining the street outside our home.

■ ■ ■

AT UNITED HOSPITAL IN Saint Paul, in 2007, I said goodbye to my grandmother. She went into the hospital with breathing problems only to find that cancer had covered her lungs and lymph nodes and she had days left to live.

One of the last things my grandmother said was directly to my mother: "Be nice to Emily, she will be the only person who stays by your side." Grandma knew that Mom was in trouble with drugs and that her other children had lost patience with their sister.

"You need to get away from your mother," my aunts and uncle would say. "Your mother can't be helped. You would be better off without her in your life." But, instead of making me run, those comments empowered me. Now, I would do whatever I could to stay by my mother's side. I would prove them all wrong.

Just after my grandmother passed away, my mother had to turn herself in to jail to serve a ninety-day sentence. Once a week, I drove to Saint Paul to visit her there. It broke my heart to think of my mother in jail but even when I visited, she was distant.

When I knew her release date was nearing, I tried to do everything I could to have her come home to some comfort and stability. She'd been suffering from addiction for so long and I wanted to be there to help her stay clean. I waited and waited for her to call to tell me I could come pick her up, but the call never came. Over and over, I called the jail to make sure they hadn't made a mistake. Maybe they had given me the wrong information; maybe her release had been delayed.

A few days later, Mom came walking through the front door. From the moment I saw her I knew she was using again. She'd been on a meth binge since her release. She looked awful. It took me back immediately to my childhood. I knew when something was wrong with Mom; my sister and I both did. Sometimes when Dad dropped us off after spending a weekend with him, we would be so mad that Mom was acting that way, we would pack up our little Smurf suitcases and walk right out the door. I don't know where we thought we were going or how we eventually ended up back at home but at ten and twelve years old, my sister and I had little tolerance for our mom's behavior.

That night, when my mother finally came home from jail, high on meth, I was angry. I spoke few words to her before leaving. I really didn't know what else I could do. She was supposed to be sober and getting her life back on track. I didn't know how to help her anymore. I was barely able to help myself. She called me many times that night and for days after, but I didn't answer. I didn't know what to do. I would listen to her messages, make sure she sounded okay and then delete them. I was devastated. I needed space from my mom. It had been only a couple of months since I'd dug in my heels and promised myself I would always be by her side but now … now, I didn't know which way to turn.

And then came the night I left work and checked my phone: twenty-eight voicemails all from my mom. I could feel my entire body get hot and I was immediately filled with overwhelming fear.

Was she really capable of taking her life?

She wouldn't pick up the phone. It seemed as if the battery had died; straight to her voicemail every time I dialed her number. I will never forget what listening to those messages was like. I had never heard her that way before. I have never been so scared.

I drove 90 miles an hour to get to her house. Tears filled my eyes, I could hardly see. The closer I got, the hotter my body was getting. I raced my car into the driveway, jumping out with it barely in park. I ran to the front door, kicking it open, vaguely hearing it slam into the wall.

There she was, sitting on the plywood living room floor with blood-stained towels all around her and a bloody knife on her lap. She was calm, nothing like the person on my voicemails. She looked up at me as I shook her, and what she said, I will never forget: "Wow, I am one fucked-up person." In this horrifying, nearly tragic, life-changing moment, the only thing we could do was laugh.

When my sister arrived, we took Mom to United Hospital. The same place her own mother had passed away just a few months prior. I think she was a little caught off-guard when she realized they were going to make her stay for a while. When she tried to sneak out of her room the security guard had to stop her and tell her she couldn't leave. But finally, she gave in and accepted the help she was going to get.

This was the beginning of a long uphill battle. Mom had been diagnosed in her forties with bipolar disorder but she'd never sought treatment for her mental illness. Self-medicating was an accepted practice in her family; she'd learned it early from her own mother. Admitting that she suffered from depression was difficult for my mom. She was too proud, too stubborn to ask for help, but now she was giving in, now she would finally get the help she needed. As much as I wanted to be by her side and help her, I knew this was a problem I couldn't solve alone.

Over the last fourteen years, we have had many struggles, many problems to solve, and many hills to climb. This journey has not been easy or comfortable, but that's life.

Seeing my mother now, sober, able to take on challenges, enjoying relief from the ghosts and demons that haunted her, makes me proud. I am proud of her and I am proud of me. We stuck together, side by side, through so many things. I love watching her be a grandmother and I love having my mom present in my life.

Traveling back through time on the journey to tell this story hasn't been easy. We've cried, we've laughed, but most important, we've grown. Through tears and laughter, we've dealt with things that had been tucked far away.

It has been amazing taking this trip with you, Mom. I have nothing but hope for our future, and I promise, without a doubt, I will always be right by your side.

AUTHOR'S NOTE

WE HAD JUST LEFT Rice Street. I could tell the trip down memory lane had been hard for Linda. So many memories flooded her mind that she struggled to get them all out. Linda talks fast and she's animated. She has this spunk about her. When she sits and speaks, she's always on the edge of her seat, and when she stands, she bounces almost off of her toes. It's remarkable, really. This woman who has seen so much, done so much, has this life left in her.

It's contagious sometimes. When I speak to Linda, I find myself energized as I leave her. Somehow, regardless of the darkness that we visit each time we talk, she brings a light to my life. One I certainly didn't see coming.

But on this day, there is only darkness as we drive south on Rice Street in Saint Paul and turn west on University. All around us as we drive, as far as we can see, is destruction. Buildings are burned and boarded; graffiti marks anything still standing. George Floyd has just been killed, and the Twin Cities have been struck by riots and unrest for days. Nothing is the same as it used to be.

It's quiet in the car. Linda doesn't say much, which, if I'm being honest, is unusual for her. I imagine she's stuck somewhere between past and present, trying to find a way to feel. Trying to figure out what is now and what was then.

I glance to my right to look at my passenger. Her eyes are wet. The lines on her face seem deeper. As I fight to stay present and take in the current events around me, I simultaneously try to rebuild the past of this remarkable woman. I know she's not here with me; she's somewhere else. Linda is far away from me, though she sits beside me now.

"I remember seeing my girls," Linda says quietly. She's looking out the passenger window as we sit at a red light.

"Where?" I say, not knowing if she's talking about her daughters or her employees.

"Here. Right here." She gestures to the intersection. "After they shut me down, there was nothing I could do. I remember driving over here and seeing my girls. Right here on the corner. They were working. Street walkers. I couldn't protect them if I wanted to." It was some combination of guilt and sadness in her voice. Regret? I wasn't sure.

"Did you take care of your girls?" I ask, wondering if she was more like a brothel mom than I had suspected.

"I did. We all did," she said. "They were always better off with us than they were on the street—no doubt about that."

"'We'?"

"The sauna owners," she says, smiling. "We had a bit of a club. We looked out for each other. If there was a girl with a pimp or something going down, we warned each other. One for all, you know?"

"Like the Better Business Bureau?" I joke. Linda laughs. She's snapped from her haze.

"You want to see where I got started?" she asks.

And with that, we're off. Back down memory lane, Linda scooting to the edge of her perch in my passenger seat while I drive us through what could only be described as the remains of Saint Paul.

As I drive, I'm struck by the annihilation of these city streets. Buildings, piles of metal, really, where buildings once stood are unidentifiable in what used to be business-lined sidewalks.

"See that right there?" Linda is pointing again, this time across my field of vision at the southwest corner of the street. "That used to be where I went for drugs."

"In the building?" I asked, knowing doctor's offices were there but confused by the way she said "drugs," rather than "prescriptions" or "medicine."

"Oh yeah," she says, "all you had to do was flash that doc,

and he would write you a script for anything you wanted. It was so easy back then."

"Turn here?" I ask, shaking my head at her memory. Sometimes the things Linda says shock me. I am so out of my own life or comfort zone that I cannot fathom the experiences of hers.

"Just a few blocks up," she says as we ease to the side of the road at Snelling and Minnehaha. There's a coffee shop and thrift store and some space owned by the nearby private university.

"This was it!" she says as she opens her door and hops out.

I rush to follow her without sacrificing my car door to a passerby. "What? What is it?" I half shout.

"Lee Lenore's," Linda announces with her arms lifted as if she's introducing someone on a stage. I'm almost waiting for a spotlight to come on. "This is where it all started. Well, not all of it, but you know that," she says.

"I do," I say, because I know Linda lived a long life before she ever got here.

■ ■ ■

To be a "Fallen Woman" means to have fallen from grace. More specifically, a "fallen woman" is said to have given away her innocence. Linda never had the opportunity to give away her innocence. Hers was taken. She was too young to offer it to the taker—he just took it. Perhaps that is what started her fall.

As she made her way through life, things stacked up on her. The weight grew heavier with each choice she made and every path she took. Linda never had anyone take the load off of her, and so it continued to grow. Her burden eventually became too much to bear, and Linda collapsed under its weight. She fell hard and far, and the landing was rough. But she got up, dusted herself off, and kept going. She decided what she wanted, and she got it. Linda has life. She has happiness and joy and all the things a person could need.

Looking at Linda, I see someone who can smile through pain and find light when there is only dark. Linda has taught me that a laugh can be contagious, even in the saddest of times.

I've never met anyone quite like Linda May Spencer. She truly is a force contained in a tiny package. She makes herself big with gigantic motions, and her voice booms to fill any space she's in. But for all her exuberance, I can see that Linda is sad. Behind the twinkle in her eyes is sorrow. She still lives with two profoundly different and conflicting sides.

You can't live a life like Linda has and not carry regret. She's done and seen too much to ever really forget, but she's worked hard to forgive herself for the mistakes that she made.

It is my hope that I've done justice to her story. That she will become an inspiration to someone else who has fallen and is trying to get up.

Linda's story is not like mine and it is probably not like yours. She's lived a life unlike any I could ever imagine. But Linda has brought light to my life. She is a testament to a person's ability to change. Proof that we aren't a reflection of our mistakes but a patchwork of our experiences, and from them we can give others hope for their own lives.

By telling her story, I hope Linda can find inspiration in herself. By seeing herself through someone else's eyes, I want her to see who she has become, rather than who she was. It is time for Linda to step out of the dark and into the light she shines on the people around her.

ACKNOWLEDGMENTS

THANK YOU IS NOT enough to express my sincere gratitude to Linda May Spencer for trusting me with her story. It has been a privilege beyond measure. Reconstructing your story has enlightened me and taught me the value in holding your ground ... even when it shakes. I do not doubt for a moment that your story will inspire others to get up.

Emily, you have endured a lifetime of uphill battles and you have conquered them all. You embody the light your mom fought so hard to reach and continue everyday to carry her and the others around you into your light.

This unbelievable story would not be what it is if it had

not been for the persistence and dedication of an amazing woman who I have never even met. Keri Kowski, you have been my silent partner in this journey. I cannot thank you enough. The City of Saint Paul is lucky to have you on their team.

To the court clerks who took the time to reopen those dusty old files — I am so grateful. You allowed me the opportunity to piece together details of a past that had been tucked away.

Without editors, authors would be lost. Thank you to Erin and Kate who took this from good to great with talents I will never posess.

■ ■ ■

When it comes to this writing journey I have a team of cheerleaders, you know who you are. You quietly build pyramids and wave pompoms all around me while I research, develop, write and pace the floor drafting sentences in my head. You read the drafts, give the tough feedback and push back when necessary. You are my team, thank you for your endless support.

To my amazing partners Alisha and Anna, this HH journey, like many in my life, started in a coffee shop and has endured a lifetime of "unprecedented," in its infancy. We've made it through that, we can make it through anything. Doyenne!

To Pat Elliott, my forever mentor and friend. You have given me the legal chops to keep doing this true crime thing. I thank you again and always.

To my guys, thank you again for giving me the space and time to write. I love you so much.

■ ■ ■

ABOUT THE AUTHOR

Allison Mann is an author, publisher and paralegal. After graduating from Winona State University in 2001, Allison began a nearly twenty-year career as a paralegal in the Twin Cities of Minnesota.

After co-authoring her first book, The Girls Are Gone, Allison found her way to the publishing world. In 2020, Allison co-founded and is the CEO of Hadleigh House Publishing where she developed the Hadleigh House Unpacked imprint.

Allison resides in the Twin Cities with her family, enjoying life as a boy mom and all that comes along with it. When she's not writing, Allison can be found getting lost in a bookstore or wandering the halls of a courthouse.

For signing, events and more go to
www.allisonmannmn.com

CPSIA information can be obtained
at www.ICGtesting.com
Printed in the USA
FSHW010034100621
82182FS